Horizontal Management

Beyond Total Customer Satisfaction

by

D. Keith Denton
Southwest Missouri State University

LEXINGTON BOOKS
An Imprint of Macmillan, Inc.
NEW YORK

Maxwell Macmillan Canada
TORONTO

Maxwell Macmillan International
NEW YORK   OXFORD   SINGAPORE   SYDNEY

Library of Congress Cataloging-in-Publication Data
Denton, D. Keith.
    Horizontal management : beyond total customer satisfaction / by D.
Keith Denton.
        p.   cm.
    Includes indexes.
    ISBN 0-669-26936-0
    1. Work groups.   2. Management—Employee participation.
3. Customer relations.   I. Title.
    HD66.D45   1991
    658.8'12—dc20   91-6845
                                                                       CIP

Lexington Books
An Imprint of Macmillan, Inc.
866 Third Avenue, New York, N. Y. 10022

Maxwell Macmillan Canada, Inc.
1200 Eglinton Avenue East
Suite 200
Don Mills, Ontario M3C 3N1

Macmillan, Inc. is part of the Maxwell Communication
Group of Companies

Printed in the United States of America

printing number
1 2 3 4 5 6 7 8 9 10

Contents

List of Figures and Tables

Figures

Tables

About the Book

Horizontal Management: Beyond Total Customer Satisfaction is a book about what could be if current trends continue. The heart of the book is divided into three parts beginning with "Serving the Customer," which describes what is occurring within some of America's most competitive and innovative organizations. Included here are descriptions of the techniques that these companies used to become competitive. Their secret is their focus on their customers.

Of course, just about everyone will tell you that the customer comes first, but if that were the case then why are there so few that back up those words with deeds, products, and services? We will see how to bring customers into both managerial thoughts and actions by structuring decision making around them. This involves rethinking the way business is organized including creating a network of communication links between internal and external customers and suppliers, and then tracking performance to see the impact of those changes.

"Beyond Customer Satisfaction" describes what is increasing the competitive advantage, namely horizontal management. The structure and managerial actions that comprise horizontal management are not one structure. Rather they can be thought of as a continuum ranging from the traditional vertical pyramid organization to a completely flat or "level one" organization. It is this section that identifies the steps needed to move toward a level one organization where there are no supervisors, at least not in the traditional sense. It then provides a multitude of examples and illustrations of companies taking significant strides in that direction.

At the center of this new philosophy is the need to redesign the way decisions are made and make better use of our people and technology. In some cases it involves making better use of technological systems like computer networks or Artificial Intelligence systems. In other cases it demands that management rethink the decision-making process and its extensive, inefficient centralization.

Today, companies of all sizes are rethinking the way decisions are made and who should make them. Included in this restructuring are new network organizations that make extensive use of the operational tool of the 1990s, team management. We will look at teams that are being used to make decisions concerning the day-to-day scheduling of work, hiring and firing, the distribution of rewards and pay, and even the financial and strategic questions once considered the exclusive province of highest-level management.

The final section addresses what can become a reality for those wanting a twenty-first-century organization now. This section, "Creating a Compeer Culture," is really about the need for creating *equity* between employees and management. In a totally equitable organization there will be neither employees nor managers, only equals—*compeers*.

This may sound far-fetched, but I have included some examples where this is already well underway. We will also see how to use *horizontal motivators* to create greater equity, empowerment, and competitiveness as well as look at some of the obstacles still in the path of these trends. We will look at how these obstacles being dealt with and draw some conclusions about what is needed to achieve level-one horizontal management.

Acknowledgments

Writing a book is always a team effort. This book would not have been possible without the help of my wife, Carolyn, who typed most of it and read every page, usually more than once, and suggested numerous improvements. I am also indebted to Anita Looney and Joanne Pijut for their word-processing abilities and perfectionist attitudes. Charles Boyd, Debbie Goodale, and Peter Richardson's reviews also greatly improved the quality of the book.

Part I
Challenges

1
Equitable Structures

S ome time ago I received a call from a casino organization. Their vice-president of human resources said he had read an article I had written about a company that was using a radical new approach to employee involvement. He said that was what his company wanted to do, "You know, *empower* our people!" I asked him how he planned to do that, and he replied, "That's the problem. We know what we want to do, but we don't know exactly how to do it."

When I pressed the point, it became obvious that despite what he said, he did not really have a problem understanding how to empower people. Instead, the problem was the fact that he (and probably the company) really did not understand *what* he wanted to do. He had no theory, no structure, no focus or direction on which to build. All he knew was that he had read about a technique that seemed to produce the kind of results he wanted. What he did not realize was that this technique like other techniques such as quality circles, just-in-time production, etc., are only as good as the support provided them by the proper organizational structure. *Techniques* can only be applied in specific situations. *Theories* create direction and a focus on which to build management actions.

If he and other managers at the casino had first decided what kind of organization they had and what kind of organizational structure they needed, he would then know what to do. It is relatively easy to determine how to accomplish a goal like employee empowerment if we create a structure that generates a renewing process. Ineffective organizations create programs; effective organizations create processes. Programs succeed or fail (mostly fail), and then are terminated. A process generates its own energy and, coincidentally, its own programs. These programs or techniques are really of only secondary importance. The program or technique this vice-president of human resources was interested in had long since been discarded by the company mentioned in the article he'd read, but the process of employee involvement at the company continued.

That is one of the challenges in trying to document the accomplishments of highly successful and dynamic organizations. When you visit them for the first time, they will explain one of their current programs (a symptom), but when you come back in a year, they no longer have the program. They do, however, have a fertile process (cause) that is constantly generating programs to meet specific purposes, which then die to make room for new programs.

The less dynamic, less successful companies will implement a program, and years later they are still using it. It may have lost its effectiveness, but it is still in place. Some even less successful companies cannot even set up a program.

Managerial impotence is what happens to managers who are looking for the quick fix, the ten steps to success or other "keep it short and simple" approaches that many management consultants use on time-poor, money-rich clients. We have all read the same stories about new techniques like quality circles, just-in-time (JIT) production, Material Requirement Planning (MRP), and Quality Function Deployment (QFD). Almost in the same breath we hear of a 70, 80, or even 90 percent failure rate using the same techniques. Why is there such a high failure rate when the technology or program seems so promising?

Square Pegs and Round Holes

Certainly, one reason for failure can be seen in management's approach to a program. I was recently contacted by a manager of operations for a sporting goods wholesaler and retailer who had gotten excited about a new program he had heard about called Total Quality Management (TQM). He had attended a one-day seminar and heard a speech about TQM and was convinced it would make his company more competitive. He wanted help in setting up a motivational seminar so he could expose his personnel to the concept. After this one-day seminar, he wanted to set up training "programs" in statistical process control (SPC) and related techniques to teach his personnel how to implement TQM.

While he was excited about TQM and obviously was willing to spend the money to teach others some of the techniques used in TQM, I would be extremely surprised if he were successful. The company he works for is known for its marketing muscle and happens to be in a high-growth market. Its use of its people is another matter. In that area his company is not so "muscular."

To give you an example, in a high-level meeting with this manager of operations, one of the other managers turned to him and in an off-the-cuff manner asked, "How long have you been here, Ed?" He answered, "Three years." The other manager responded, "Well, I guess that makes you an 'old timer.'" The manager of operations smiled and said, "Yes, it does."

The trouble with this company and others like it that fail to achieve results from such programs is often the unsatisfactory climate. At this company and others like it the turnover is high, the environment is political, infighting is frequent, disenchantment is common, and nine-tenths of their human potential is wasted. Otherwise innovative programs fail to achieve their potential because of a failure to build a proper foundation or structure. Until the manager of operations addresses the issue of how decisions are made, and how they go about doing business, no amount of excitement, money, or effort will help. This was summed up by Hal Sperlich, president of Chrysler Corporation from 1984 to 1988 and a twenty-year veteran of Ford Motor Company, who said, "For decades manufacturing facilities have been adjusted, added to, modified or misused in our effort to squeeze the square peg through the round hole."[1] The same thing has happened with organizational structures.

It is this type of square-peg manager who reads about the "one-minute manager" and really believes it is that simple. How would you like to go to a doctor who reads the "One-Minute Physician"? Granted, management is not rocket science, but it is outrageous to think that in one minute you can change anything. That is pop psychology at its worst. There are no simple solutions to complex problems like restructuring organizations, and failure to maximize human potential. To create round pegs and engage the work force is a complex *process*.

Crisis management is applying techniques with little thought to how to fit these techniques with the normal organizational process. In the previous example, TQM is a philosophy or process that requires greater delegation, greater sharing of power, greater equality, and greater development of people. Until a company starts treating its employees better and more equitably, TQM simply cannot take root.

This book shows an approach that can give structure to management decisions. It suggests a framework for making decisions, for involving employees in a logical and rational way. Nothing is quite as useful as a good theory, and it provides a theory around which to organize empowerment efforts. It is written for those who want direction and not just reaction. It is for those who want to empower their people but do not know how to do it systematically.

Structure and Strategy

In many ways, the present concern over empowerment reminds me of accident control. One of the first jobs I held was that of safety engineer. I was then and still am amazed at traditional accident investigation and control. For instance, there might be an increasing incidence in a plant of back injuries. A supervisor or safety engineer would investigate the problem and follow up the investigation with recommendations for solving it. Sure enough, with enough effort, management attention, and money, the incidence of that particular type of problem would decrease. Did that mean accident investigators were out of business? Hardly. Some other problem would crop up involving machinery, property, or some other area. That new problem would then draw management's attention, and the cycle would repeat—an investigation, an identification of symptoms (although we called them "causes"), and a reaction of some sort by management.

In much the same way, organizational management seems to go from one crisis to another. One moment it is some overhead cost, market position, or, the current rage, quality and customer satisfaction. Management recognizes a problem, investigates the symptoms, applies a technique or two, and throws money at it until the next "hot button" occurs. In short, there are no long-term solutions, only short-term reactions.

Like accidents, each of these managerial crises is only a symptom of larger structural problems. This book suggests a way of restructuring organizations *horizontally* to eliminate the underlying problem rather than just treat its symptoms. First though, let us look at some of the current incidents that are creating increasing pressure for change. The need for change is there. Whether we simply react through crisis management or make fundamental changes in the way work is organized will determine our long-term success.

Dysfunctional Organizations

There are those who design products and services and there are those who are responsible for producing them so they can be consumed by the customer. You would think it would be a natural collaboration. Unfortunately, the relationship between product designers and process and production managers is one of our oldest running gags. Usually the joke is in reference to product designers tossing it (the design) over the wall (to production people) so they can then figure out how they can adapt the design so they can product the item.

It may be an old joke, but no one is laughing anymore. Product designers and production people are not the only culprits. Marketing doesn't seem to understand what the customer wanted in the first place. The communication links among all these functional areas are inadequate. At one time we tolerated such inefficiencies; it even helped justify the employment of managerial "firemen" who went from crisis to crisis, "putting out fires."

Today things are different. We cannot afford such "featherbedding." If we do not do a better job of coordinating, designing, manufacturing, and delivering products and services, our customers will simply look for someone who will. There are some fascinating organizations worldwide that have turned the closer linking of their functional areas into a competitive advantage.

The problem with product, process, and customer interaction is within the very structure of organizations. Typically, marketing, product designers, and production people are at different echelons within an organization. It is not natural for them to interact, let alone understand, each other. It is only when these divergent groups are equally involved in the production process that you end up with goods that are both producible and profitable.

The reason why it is so hard for us to deliver goods and services that are both easy to produce and profitable rests in the fact that American firms tend to be organized around hierarchies resembling the military model. In this case, the CEO is the general, supported by a cadre of managerial officers organized pyramidally. Those working in this pyramid of power work at different levels with different perspectives. Formal communication in this context is vertical, from boss to subordinate.

Decision making resembles those electric circuits connected in a series. The energy must move from one point to the next in a fixed sequence. As such, vertical pyramid organizations tend to be heavily bureaucratic, isolated, and rigid. Each step in the series is haunted by concerns of self-protection, politics, and manipulation. This is the true legacy of the pyramid. This has helped erode our manufacturing base. Even for those working in services, this straightjacket has become a serious challenge to our standard of living.

Erosion of Our Manufacturing Base

Some years ago an MIT study titled "Work In America" noted that America has to pay more attention to manufacturing if it hopes to regain a competitive edge. Many would agree that managers spend most of their time buying things; they are more interested in mergers and acquisitions rather than in building on what they have. In order for the American manufacturing base to become more competitive, it has to get better at making things, as measured against the best in the world.

One hears a lot of talk about "buy American," but what we should be saying is "sell American." Our products should be world class; good enough to compete with anyone's. Those that are not should be brought up to par or eliminated so we can focus in areas where we are competitive.

In addressing the cause of America's failure to compete in the manufacturing sector, the MIT commission calls on U.S. executives to rethink how they hire and manage their work force. Using the highly successful high-wage textiles industries of Japan, Italy, and Germany as models, the commission faults the untiring efforts of American managers to squeeze out the most work for the least pay. The real key is to train and motivate workers to fully utilize today's sophisticated machinery.[2]

As a nation, we are losing our world domination in manufacturing not so much because of the emergence of Pacific Rim countries nor unfavorable monetary exchange rates, but because of our inability to make the best use of our most valuable resource—our people. We are still trying to use early twentieth-century techniques for a twenty-first-century world. Companies may profess the importance of the customer, but until they build organizations around them, customers will remain an outside factor. Lip service does not count; it is deeds that matter. The customer must be ingrained into the very structure of the organization. Still, ways are being found to create a more cooperative atmosphere within companies as well as between companies and their suppliers. We have to begin to develop ways where all organizational members—production people, accountants, marketers and designers, and others—work better together and are more focused on a single direction.

As with the lack of communication between product and process designers, problems are almost always multidisciplinary, so why aren't our businesses organized around a system designed to encourage more peer problem solving? Joint decision making and greater delegation of authority, responsibility, and accountability to lower levels are going to be essential to resolving the problems of dysfunctional organizations. One way of doing this is to ensure that employees gain experience in and learn to take responsibility in a variety of areas in a firm. Currently, companies like D.E.C., Boeing, and others are enhancing their manufacturing base by doing exactly that. Some companies start their M.B.A.s and entry-level engineers on the factory floor. This gives them a good start at understanding company operations from a variety of perspectives. Continuous cross-training is a critical component for world-class competitors.

Global Competitiveness

Our eroding manufacturing base is really part of a much larger problem. This erosion is obviously due to not being able to sustain our own productivity in the face of increasing competition. Some blame the Japanese or the Germans. Some blame a poor work ethic or poor attitude. Some complain of not having a level playing field because of unfair trading practices overseas. Incidentally, we will not get a very sympathetic ear in the world community on this one. A survey conducted by a highly respected European research institute cited six of the twenty-three member nations of the Organization for Economic Cooperation and Development (OECD) as unfair traders. The three worst offenders were Japan, Korea, and the

United States. It is a fact that 30 percent of our goods are protected by import duties and quotas.

Attempting to pass the blame is a symptom that obscures the larger problem, namely our lack of productivity and competitiveness. Those who propose the short and simple solution of "buy American" are missing the point. Why do people buy foreign? Could it be that foreign products are simply cheaper and better? Until that changes, there can be no long-term solution to our lack of competitiveness. Our focus should be to "sell American." We have to benchmark ourselves against world competitors, not American ones. The conclusion of the "Made in America" report by MIT's commission on Industrial Productivity was that, "American industry is not producing as well as it ought to produce or as well as it used to produce or as well as the industries of some other nations have learned to produce."[3]

Until we address this fundamental issue, things will only worsen. We have a $600 billion debt and that is due to a lack of competitiveness. Compared to Brazil's $120 billion and Mexico's $105 billion, we are major-league debtors. Is there any wonder why many worry how long our creditors will continue to support us?

Of the fifty largest banks in the world, forty-seven are *not* American. The six largest are Japanese. As the trade surpluses with the United States have grown, so too has the number of dollars foreigners put back into this country. "The interest rate you pay for a car or mortgage now depends greatly on the attitudes and actions of investors and policymakers in Japan. That is why the Treasury Department worries more when Nippon Life Insurance fails to show up for a government bond auction than it does about The Travelers or Prudential. Japanese financial institutions have allowed Americans to run mammoth budget deficits and yet avoid economic disaster.[4]

In some cases, we are not competitive; in other cases, we do not even try to compete. According to the Price Waterhouse Information Guide, nearly forty thousand American companies could profitably export their products to the rest of the world, but do not.[5]

Tunnel vision, an exclusive focus on the American market, not only hurts our general productivity, but is creating a situation where we are missing opportunities to compete. The American perspective of high volume and mass production may have been fine in a more homogeneous climate, but today we are world citizens and it is time that we located our place in the global society.

Highly structured societies with distinct divisions of class, status, and position will be at a disadvantage in a world where everyone expects, even demands, more respect for his or her opinions and needs. This atmosphere of equality is in direct contrast to the old, hierarchial attitude that says,

"It is not enough that I have it; it is that you don't have it." Worldwide competitiveness demands a more flexibility. American managers and corporations more concerned with pecking order, perks, pay differentials, and the corporate pyramid rather than the people are curiously out of date.

If we are going to be competitive, it will depend on our people. We have to bring our people into the process to make them full partners if we hope to engage our work force. It is no longer acceptable to let some "fly second class."

Those Damned Employees

Maybe it is a little strong, but many at the highest level blame those at the lowest level for our current lack of competitiveness. Either they are too young, too inexperienced, too unmotivated, too uneducated, or simply too uncaring. Every operational manager has his or her pet peeve. In fact, a survey of industrial engineers reported that 78.5 percent either strongly agreed or somewhat agreed that there was a lack of a strong work ethic.[6] These productivity specialists believe this lack of a strong work ethic is contributing to our lower productivity. No one asks why do workers not care? Why are they so turned off from work?

Certainly their managerial counterparts have a low regard for their employees' aptitudes. According to the MIT commission cited earlier, American managers underestimate the importance of education and training. After two years of study and 550 interviews with various industries, the commission found a curious result. They did not find a single U.S. industry representative who considered the educational qualifications of workers to be a significant factor in productivity. In contrast, Italian, Japanese and German textile and apparel executives told of process and product innovations that would not be possible without skilled, highly educated workers able to exercise initiative. Perhaps it is not the work ethic that is important. Rather, it is education and treatment of those workers that are the important factors.

Disenchantment with work does not have to be. Consider an employee named Lisa. Lisa spends long hours working on a production floor, wearing unflattering surgical hairnets and mud-colored rubber boots, making about $20,000 a year, and never getting two days off in a row. Know what? She loves it! Why? One of the reasons is the fact that she chooses which production task she will do each day. Every day she runs the risk of getting a free back rub or having a hilarious run-in with the company's "Joy Gang." Every day 7.5 percent of her company's pre-tax profits go to a worthy social cause, like the environment, that she helps choose. She also has benefits like free health club membership, profit sharing, and college tuition.[7] Most want to work and contribute. The problem is not the lack of a work ethic, but the lack of work equity.

Equity

Thomas J. Watson, Jr., former CEO of IBM, made the point that "the real difference between success and failure in a corporation can very often be traced to the question of how well the organization brings out the great energies and talents of its people."[8] Those thoughts expressed the early 1960s are even more true in today's environment of global competitiveness and greater customer expectations. Just when management is most in need of great efforts from the entire work force, it seems that that work force is disintegrating.

Even experienced employees and seasoned middle managers seem to be losing their grip on the oars. For many, there is a growing disillusionment with work. Jack Stack, *INC* magazine's "Dream Team" CEO and president of the highly successful Springfield Remanufacturing Company (SRC), which was featured in the PBS special "Grow Your Own Business," notes that for many employees and managers in business today "there is no finish line." They keep trying to go upstream and they do not know why. They tire, pause to look up, and get carried downstream by the current. On the other hand, he believes that if they knew why they needed to row upstream, they might row even harder. While Stack and his team may not have trouble getting more effort from their people, plenty of managers are.

Employees are outraged by the difference between their pay and perks and those of their CEOs. Bruce Pfau, executive vice-president of Sirota Alper & Pfau, randomly surveyed 350 employees nationwide. He discovered that two-thirds of those employees thought the CEO got too big a share of corporate profits. Nearly half believed their own share was about right, and a solid majority believed the shares going to stockholders, to the community at large, and to reinvestment was also about right.[9] Only top management was perceived to be getting more than it deserved.

Since 1979 the gap between top management's compensation and the compensation of workers has grown wider and wider. CEOs with one hundred times the salary of line employees are not uncommon.[10] How serious is this pay discrepancy? In *Fortune* magazine, Peter Drucker notes that poorly performing organizations had one characteristic in common. "Each company's top executive was paid more than 130 percent of the compensation of the people in the next echelon, and these in turn, more than 130 percent of the compensation of those below them." The conclusion is that disproportionately high executive salaries disrupt teamwork. So what is a more reasonable proportion? There is a formula. Peter Drucker recommends a twenty-to-one ratio between the highest and lowest salary in an organization. Socrates endorsed a five-to-one ratio.[11]

Is Anyone Out There Listening?

Pay, golden parachutes, and other perks given only to a privileged few are not the main problem. There have always been perks, and there will always be gaps in status. Rather, it is how supervisors, professionals, technical and clerical personnel, and middle managers perceive the atmosphere within the typical company that is the problem. These people, along with the hourly employees, increasingly believe that top management is distant and unresponsive.

The Opinion Research Corporation of Chicago surveyed 100,000 middle managers, supervisors, professionals, salespeople, and technical, clerical, and hourly employees of the Fortune 500 companies. They found that, except for sales personnel, everyone else, including middle management, thought upper management was less willing to listen to them now than they were just five years earlier. They also believed top management gave them less respect than in the past.[12]

There may be some truth to those beliefs. Foster Higgins & Co., an employee-benefits consulting firm, finds only 45 percent of large employers make regular use of worker opinion surveys.[13] If employers are not even doing this simple auditing process, is there any wonder that the work force and managers below the highest level feel that they are not being heard? Examine the absenteeism, turnover, apathy, hostility, and even physical sabotage and hostility many feel toward their organizations. Add to this the fact that in a survey of 206 CEOs of Fortune 500 companies, 77 percent said that U.S. companies will have to push their managers harder if we, as a nation, are to compete successfully with the Japanese and other global competitors.[14]

It is clear that serious problems can occur when top executives are saying their work force will need to row harder to deliver the customer service, innovations, and competitiveness we will need in the future. Meanwhile, they are lecturing to an increasingly sullen, dispirited crew suffering from low morale, burnout, and distrust of management motives.

Seeds of a Solution

How do we get our people to assume more responsibility, take risks, assume accountability, focus on quality, concentrate on customers, and make better decisions? Jack Stack makes the point that we have all these really smart people. They all went through the right training programs; some obtained the highest position with great responsibilities. Despite knowing more than anyone else about their jobs, they are not allowed to participate in terms of *equity*. It is natural for people to really begin to question their own worth when they do not feel there is equity within the company— when they do not have a sense of "ownership" about the organization. Everyone within any organization has this same need.

In meeting this need it is not so much what is done but how it is done. Profit sharing, gainsharing, and other incentives plans are examples of managerial tools that ought to work but frequently do not. Jude Rick, president of Sibson and Co., a human-resource consulting firm, estimates that $125 billion is spent by U.S. firms on employee incentives that do not work. Other experts say roughly half of current incentive plans do not work. Perhaps that is why when the Public Agenda Foundation surveyed 845 white- as well as blue-collar workers they found that fully 45 percent of them do not believe there is a link between pay and performance.[15]

Stack observes that people are always asking how his company, SRC, keeps its employees so engaged. He notes that what they really want is to be able to go back and convince their boss to let them have more of a say in what goes on. For example, one publisher operated a profit-sharing system, but the people within the company had no access to financial information they needed to determine how to improve those profits. While marketing and sales may have a tremendous knowledge about market share, they have no concept of cost. When they ordered a market test, proofs, galleys, or other action, they had no idea of what it was costing— and yet they were on a bonus program! The point is, how can you be on a profit-sharing program and not know what you are doing in terms of making profits and controlling costs? Without a thorough understanding of the income statement and balance sheet, profit sharing is a bad joke.

Focus on Causes, Not Symptoms

People, Stack would agree, are intelligent. Many of them come up against a brick wall and say, "I can't go any further." It is a wall built by management. Stack says workers then find themselves saying, "You are not giving me the tools to go any further!" The result is these people end up thinking, "That's it! I'm dropping out; I'm burned out—it's no longer interesting." People can get to the point where they are making big salaries and can even influence what they are doing but still be unhappy because they cannot influence anything else.

At SRC people feel empowered because upper management takes out the frustrations and creates interest and motivation. They do this by giving their people more than the physical tools to do a job. They give them the intellectual tools to do their jobs, intellectual tools to make good decisions.

Stack emphasizes that there are big differences between the physical and intellectual aspects of a job. People need to see that they are improving to believe they are achieving. They need to be reinforced on a daily basis that what they are doing is contributing to something.

Losing sight of the horizon (and it is easy to do when you are low on the pyramid) and not knowing where you are heading is not strictly a problem for those on the lower decks. With highly bureaucratic organization and excessive division of labor, everyone, regardless of rank, can feel adrift. Anyone, including managers, can get to the point where they ask themselves "How can I make all this money and have all this responsibility and yet not be trusted with information to do my job?" Stack believes people frequently find themselves asking, "Why am I doing it (work) for *them*?" As a result, they burn out because they are working and giving the company everything and getting nothing to show for it.

Parity

The principle reason why companies suffer the symptoms of lack of competitiveness, customer dissatisfaction, and employee problems and why even managers often feel frustrated and burned out is, according to SRC's CEO, due to a lack of trust. Trust, as Stack says, is a two-way street. Most of the problems today between management and the work force are because of lack of trust—either you (the worker) are not getting it or you (the manager) are not giving it.

Tom Peters notes that SRC creates an atmosphere of trust by sharing financial information with all employees. As he notes, "When people are privy to the numbers (where they come from, what they mean, how the individual influences them), miracles of engagement, commitment, and contribution occur.[16]

Trust is built on management's recognition of the work force and on honest relationships and communication between senior managers and employees. In short, trust is built on *equity* (there's that word again!) within the organization. To become more competitive and engage an increasingly disengaged work force will require greater fairness within the organization if it, as Thomas J. Watson, Jr., says, is to "bring out the great energy and talents of its people."

There are many things that can be done. The philosophy used by SRC of tying the financial interests of upper management and lower-level work force closer together is one obvious way. Each one's risks and rewards must be more equitable. Gainsharing, profit sharing, or other similar programs are a good start provided those people can actually have some control and understanding of costs.

SRC goes well beyond simple profit sharing. They operate an Employee Stock Ownership Plan (ESOP) and teach everyone from janitors to supervisors basic understanding of the income statement and balance sheet. They are also completely honest about where expenses, assets, and debts are occurring. Every week, upper management goes over the income statement line by line with their managers who in turn review costs, gross margins, favorable and unfavorable variances, purchase prices, sales forecasts, and so forth. Other activities include drawing up corporation-wide commodity budgets that help them develop a better corporate perspective. A generous incentive program that focuses on meeting corporate goals rather than individual incentives, which can make people greedy, are further ways of creating workplace equity.

Rank Has Its Privileges

Workplace equity and work-force trust are enhanced when perks and status symbols and, most important, true power distributions between organizational levels are reduced. Perks reward—they also distract and punish. Oriental rugs, private parking, corner offices, mahogany desks, even office sizes based on rank are destructive because they focus everyone's efforts on securing the trappings of status rather than teamwork. When Union Carbide moved into their new headquarters, they implemented a more uniform, egalitarian approach, including no executive parking or special dining room. Did it work? Yes, according to those in charge, all measures of productivity went up. As one might assume, SRC headquarters offices are very Spartan compared to most corporate headquarters.

More important than the superficial perks is the atmosphere of equality that exists in an organization. Organizations that project equity have a sense of family. There is frequent contact with the entry-level echelon. Soliciting employee suggestions, formal and informal employee surveys, and developing closer communications are all part of creating a closer family atmosphere.

At SRC there is a bond between lower and upper levels because the organization does a great job, among other things, of cross-training with the objective that each employee develop a deep understanding of all aspects of the business. Other companies are also using innovative ways of keeping in touch with the operational level. Companies like Hyatt Hotels and Southland Corporation (the 7-Eleven people) have their corporate people spend time each year working side by side with lower-level workers. Hyatt's corporate staff actually spend time changing sheets and running elevators, among other activities. Southland's corporate vice-presidents have worked behind the counters in their 7-Eleven convenience stores. It may sound corny, but it is important for organizations to keep a down-in-the-trenches perspective. It is also important for those in the trenches to know their headquarters staff is composed of real people, not managerial cyborgs.

There is a growing discontent in our work force, not only at the ground level but up through much of the rank and file. Whenever this occurs, it is serious, but it is much more so now with an increasing labor shortage. This growing discontent is happening while there is a growing need for better customer service and a growing demand that we become globally competitive.

It is becoming clear that in order to prevent burnout, apathy, and discontent in the work force, management must focus on employee relations as never before. It is the key to our future competitiveness.

Concluding Thoughts

Developing and engaging our work force means creating a more equitable work place; one where there is real ownership. Remember the trade deficit discussed earlier. Well, "over half of our trade deficit now comes from foreign industries that pay their workers higher wages than we do," emphasizes Ira Magazine, a Providence management consultant. They don't beat us with cheap labor. They beat us with technology and skilled labor.[17] We have to engage that work force. As we shall see in future chapters, there are many ways of doing this; we have already looked at one way.

SRC engages its work force with almost complete openness about financial aspects of their business. Stack says that SRC empowers their employees by giving them the opportunity to improve profits by providing employees with the financial numbers to be able to make decisions.

For SRC, *equity*, the unifying factor, is primarily obtained through extensive use of the income statement. If ten thousand people completely understand the income statement, at least they have one thing in common. However valuable the income statement is, it is not enough.

At SRC management knows profit structure, but it also focuses on communicating, on keeping in touch, and it is honest, open, and forthright with the work force. Once when I asked a line employee if he really understood all of these financial figures he was given he said, "Not really." So I asked him why he worked so hard and was so loyal to the company. He simply said, "Well, I guess I just trust them."

You cannot put a price tag on that kind of trust and respect. While not all companies may want to be as open with or treat their ground-level people with the respect SRC does, there are things any company can do to enhance equity and motivation. Look at pay and perks. Most importantly, look at the way work is organized. Do employees keep their own hours, keep records on their productivity, fix their own equipment, or meet with suppliers or interview recruits on their own? Look at how often management communicates with the work force. Is there an incentive to work? If so, is it focused on greed or cooperation? Do employees have control over those things that can affect the bottom line and, most importantly, do they understand that?

To engage the work force upper management must realistically evaluate the fairness and impartiality within the organization. If you are going to ask people to put their backs into it, is there a reason for them to feel it is for them as well as for you? Do they know what and where the finish line is or is it just mindless rowing?

In future chapters we will look at a structure that one can use to implement these changes in a realistic way, but first we need to examine the forces that are directly flattening the pyramid. These are some of the reasons why Tom Peters notes smart companies are quickly moving from narrow, vertical organizations to a broad, project-oriented, horizontal approach.[18]

Notes

1. "Industry Leader on U.S. Competition: We Are Outmanaged," *Industrial Engineering* 22, no. 6 (June 1990), p. 9.

2. Rahul Jacob, "How to Regain the Productive Edge," *Fortune*, 22 May 1989, pp. 92–93.

3. Ibid., p. 93.

4. Bill Powell and Martin Bradley, "What Japan Thinks of Us," *Newsweek*, 2 April 1990, p. 19.

5. "You Too Can Become An Exporter," *Research and Development*, June 1986, p. 25.

6. "Productivity and Quality Survey," *Focus: Industrial Engineering*, April 1990, p. 6.

7. Carol Clurman, "More Than Just A Paycheck," *USA Weekend*, 19–21 January 1990, p. 1.

8. Thomas J. Watson, Jr., *A Business and Its Beliefs* (New York: McGraw-Hill, 1963), p. 4.

9. Alan Farnham, "The Trust Gap," *Fortune*, 4 December 1989, pp. 62.

10. Ibid., p. 75.

11. Ibid., p. 74.

12. Ibid., p. 57.

13. Ibid., p. 57.

14. Sally Solo, "Stop Whining and Get Back to Work," *Fortune*, 12 March 1990, p. 49.

15. Nancy J. Perry, "Here Come Richer, Riskier Pay Plans," *Fortune*, 19 December 1988, p. 51.

16. Tom Peters, "Learning to Love Change Key in Managers in '90s," *Springfield News Leader,* 18 June 1990, p. 1.

17. Otis Port, "Back to Basics," *Business Week Special,* 1989, pp. 16.

18. Peters, "Learning to Love Change."

2
Flattening the Pyramid

O bviously, there are dramatic changes occurring worldwide: Europe in 1992, the opening of the Eastern block, the failure of Communism, oil wars. It goes on and on, but there is one change occurring that may not be as newsworthy, but nevertheless it affects us daily and directly. In fact, few things will affect our daily lives as much as the flattening of organizational pyramids. It will affect not only the way we do work, but also how we interact with each other, how we treat others, and how we think of work and organizations.

For most of the twentieth century, organizational life revolved around the hierarchy. Things are changing so rapidly that history someday may classify the end of the twentieth century as the beginning of the end of the pyramid organization. If not, it will at least be the birth of a variety of alternatives to our traditional hierarchies. The legitimacy of these simplistic organizations with each level having more power, money, and control than the level below it is coming under increasing attack.

Symptoms of problems are everywhere. Many of the traditional vertical or pyramidal organizations remain bloated with middle managers. Most of these top-heavy, bureaucratic organizations are unable to respond to rapid changes needed in today's world. Long lines of communication, narrow spans of control, far too much apathy, inattention to quality, and lack of responsiveness are common. Productivity, quality, and cost control simply have not kept pace.

It is a buyer's market in that our customers have the widest possible selection. If our organizations fail to meet their needs, someone else's will. Expectations have risen and needs are constantly changing. There is a broader range of customers. We must recognize that we are part of a worldwide consumer system.

Changes

Anyone can tell that changes are occurring in the way organizations are being run. What we may not realize is that the design and structure of organizations are also changing. Whether it is by forethought or through gradual evolution, things are changing. Pyramids are flattening. Both the number of levels and the distance between levels is growing smaller. This flattening of the pyramid is not by chance. There are strong forces at work changing work relationships. In the future those who most rapidly adapt to those changes will be in the best competitive position.

Tom Peters, coauthor of *In Search of Excellence,* years ago said he had observed three factors that excellent companies possessed. These were a bias for action, closeness to the customer, and high productivity through people.[1] By this statement he meant excellent companies have an ability to move quickly and to continuously innovate in providing service and products for their customers. These companies listened to what people wanted, and they treated employees with dignity and expected them to contribute. Sounds like pretty sound advice. All of these qualities are excellent organizational goals, but few achieve those goals.

Those companies that Peters called "excellent," others might call "competitive." Regardless of the term one uses companies that can innovate quickly and can get maximum effort out of their people are rare. Those who do it, do it because they simply have a better system of management. When a company is not "excellent," not "competitive," it is usually not the fault of the employee or the managers. It is the system.

In reference to Peters's earlier remarks about excellent companies, years later he was asked to discuss the challenges facing companies in the 1990s. Number one on his list was the end of the hierarchy.[2] He pointed out that printing firms like Quad/Graphics and better-known companies like Wal-Mart, The Limited, and Benetton beat their competition by having *very flat organizations.*

Peters goes on to say that [effective] organizations are fast becoming networks rather than pyramids. Peter Drucker believes that the manufacturing facility of the future will be a "flotilla" consisting of modules centered either around a stage in the production process or around a number of closely related operations.[3] He also believes it will be organized by its internal informational networks.

Leading thinkers and innovative leaders believe a flattening or metamorphosis is rapidly occurring. They believe it is a competitive necessity. We can begin to look at some of the factors that are causing organizations to flatten.

Need for Speed

The necessity not only for change but a change to a flatter organization comes from a variety of directions including a need for speed. Competitive organizations have a need for speed for a variety of reasons.

Technology of all types is in a constant state of change. Computer-aided design, computer-aided manufacturing, computer-integrated manufacturing, robots, bar codes, and expert systems are changing the way decisions are made and who makes them. They are even eliminating the need for many decisions.

Global competition has come to our front doorstep. Geographical distances do not relieve us of the requirement to get goods and services to customers quickly. No longer are we simply facing other American competitors using various forms of the same American management model. There are world competitors. Other nations have their own approaches, and some of these are obviously very effective.

In the previous chapter the escalating need for ever-faster product cycles was mentioned. Most of us know the value of getting our goods and services to our customers, but many do not understand just how important it is. Quickly developing, making, and distributing products and services brings important, sometimes even surprising, competitive benefits. Market share grows because customers love getting their orders *now.* "Inventories of finished goods shrink because they are not necessary to ensure quick delivery; the fastest manufacturing can make and ship an order the day it is received."[4]

Job Categories. Achieving speed means rethinking every aspect of business including our organizational structure. In our quest for speed, technology will be part of the answer, but the other part will be human. Cross-training could be the human side of the answer. There are several examples where this is occurring at different levels throughout organizations.

At the lowest operational level, General Motors has improved its speed and efficiency by loosening up job categories. Another example of where this occurred was in 1986 when United Steelworkers consolidated seventy-eight jobs into sixteen. The result was greater speed. They can now produce a ton of steel in 4.53 manhours versus 5.5 in 1984.[5]

As is often the case when there is improvement in one area, it affects other areas. Motorola provides one such case. When they reduced the number of job classifications, they not only improved their speed, but also resolved critical quality problems with their cellular telephones. When Motorola overhauled its compensation system to reward those who learned a variety of skills, their "defect rate fell 77 percent, from 1000 per million parts in 1985 to today's (1989) 233."[6]

Layers. The American pattern of having layer on layer of management is slow and unresponsive. Having five or fewer levels is fairly common in Japan. It is only in the United States that there are as many as ten or twelve levels of management. As we will see, it is not only the Japanese who have lowered organizational levels and increased speed. As often is the case, some impressive examples of this innovation in organization can be found in the United States. One of these impressive examples is Brunswick Corporation.

Brunswick Corporation is a Fortune 500 company with over 22,000 employees. It is a diversified company which serves a number of recreational and defense/aerospace markets.

In 1982, it avoided a hostile takeover. Out of this crisis came a new decentralization strategy designed to enable Brunswick to make better use of its human resources. Jack Reichert, the CEO, eliminated the function of Chief Operating Officer (COO) as well as other top executives. He consolidated eleven divisions into eight and cut the corporate staff from 560 to 220. By 1988, the corporate staff had been further reduced to 185 despite a tripling of sales. Reichert streamlined the reporting channels so that there were only five layers between him and his lowest-level employees.[7] Brunswick increased the decision-making authority at the operating-division level because as Reichert says, it was "where people knew best what to do and could do it quickly."[8] In keeping with this approach, he significantly increased the capital authority of each operating division from $25,000 to $250,000.

The result of this reorganization has been a return on their shareholder equity of around 20 percent. From 1983 to 1988, Brunswick's common stock has been the tenth fastest growing stock at the NYSE.[9]

General Electric assembled a team of manufacturing, design, and marketing specialists at its Salisbury, North Carolina, plant to make changes and improve productivity. G.E. recognized that solving problems and making decisions on the factory floor was essential to remaining competitive. "The solution was to get rid of all line supervisors and quality inspectors, reducing the organizational layers between workers and the plant manager from three to one.[10] What G.E. discovered to their delight was that the more responsibility they gave the workers, the faster problems were solved.

G.E.'s and Brunswick's solutions are only a small part of the story. Later, we will look at how other organizations are able to peel away managerial layers and gain both speed and competitiveness.

Organizations without Walls

Eliminating layers of management can be effective, but it certainly is not the only way to gain speed. Another way is to eliminate the walls or barriers separating departments or other functional areas of an organization. Ingersoll-Rand, a $3 billion machinery and equipment organization, is a perfect example of this. As noted in the first chapter, one of the keys to competitiveness is product development. It is of intense concern to CEOs. In a survey of four hundred chief executives by United Research Company, shortening product-development cycles was mentioned as their top priority.[11] Jack Reichert, CEO of Brunswick, voiced the feeling of many CEOs when he said, "Product development was like elephant intercourse. It was accompanied by much hooting, hollering and throwing of dirt, and then nothing would happen for a year."[12] The trouble is that product development often takes even longer than that for many companies.

Ingersoll-Rand provides a fairly typical situation. For them, product development often took three to four years. James D. Stryker, head of their business development, was put in charge of the task of creating an air grinder. He was unhappy with their long product-development cycles and decided to do something about it.

He felt that their long cycles were, in part, due to a succession of walls. He made reference to the old joke about marketing thinking up a product then throwing it over the wall to engineering, who in turn would come up with a design and toss it over the organizational wall to manufacturing. In turn manufacturing would send it back to sales, then sales would try to sell it to the customer who probably did not want it in the first place.[13] Nothing ever flowed smoothly; each department often accused the others of lunacy or worse.

Stryker and Ingersoll-Rand wanted to develop their products in about a year rather than the three or four years it usually took. In order to do this, they would have to avoid the problems associated with the normal product-development process. Stryker did this by creating a product-development team consisting of personnel from marketing, engineering, and manufacturing. He then developed a road map or series of steps on a chart that described the process of product development. This helped keep everyone focused on the project.

He also tried to keep them from getting distracted. One way he did this was to keep top management informed, but out of the operation.

Things did not always go smoothly. The members of the team had to learn how to communicate with and understand each other. They had to learn new perspectives. They talked to their customers and their distributors. They learned to compromise everything but their standards of quality. Despite the compromises and conflicts, they still met their goals. Their grinder even earned an award from the Industrial Design Society of America.

With these results it is not surprising that Ingersoll-Rand has expanded its product-development process. Other companies undoubtedly will follow. Tom Peters believes this horizontal project orientation of working across functional barriers will be the way business will be done in the future.[14] Speed is a competitive advantage—maybe a necessity. Flattening the pyramid by developing horizontal problem-solving networks is one way to get that speed, but speed alone is not the only reason pyramids are flattening.

Quality Competitiveness

Along with speed, quality is how companies are measuring their world-wide competitiveness. Jack Grayson, founder and chairman of the American Productivity and Quality Center, says business must recognize this reality of worldwide economic competition. To stay competitive, Grayson said American companies need to offer the highest quality they can produce, empower employees to make decisions, change systems to improve productivity, and spend more time on training.[15]

Many managers do recognize the importance of quality and they are trying to implement quality philosophies like Total Quality Management (TQM), referred to in Chapter 1. TQM is more a philosophy than an operating method. Hewlett-Packard, along with other innovative companies, uses its own form of TQM. Management at Hewlett-Packard believe it encourages continuous process improvement, universal participation in quality, and customer satisfaction as well as meeting or exceeding (internal and external) customer expectations.

Another organization implementing TQM is Bethlehem Steel. The CEO, Walt Williams, was asked how he planned to implement TQM. He said that it would consist of increasing the awareness of quality and the cost of poor quality. He went on to say that "we need to constantly monitor the progress at the *horizontal level,* the product and process level, and do a better job of communicating to each other the strategic and business plan objectives that affect quality."[16]

Williams also notes that there is an ongoing need to provide employee training to help identify areas for continuous improvement associated with TQM. Finally, he echoes the opinion of others implementing TQM when he says that they plan to use teams because quality takes the "collective efforts" of all employees working together as a team.

Throughout this discussion of TQM there are references to the need for employee involvement and support. The greater the involvement and decision making at the lowest level, the better the quality of the results. One effective decision-making tool that has been used effectively with TQM is statistical process control (SPC). SPC is a statistical technique for improving quality. Operators use control charts and sampling procedures to monitor, evaluate, and upgrade their own output. Rather than having the ultimate responsibility for quality resting with inspection or quality control departments, it rests with the operator.

Although SPC improves quality, its greatest impact "is on the factory's social organization" according to Peter Drucker.[17] Drucker goes on to say Japan's major productivity gains are the result of social changes brought on by their use of SPC. One cannot effectively implement SPC without real delegation of decision making to the lowest level. Operational employees must see quality as their responsibility and must believe that they have the authority to exercise that responsibility.

Peter Drucker emphasizes that tools like quality circles and SPC were invented in the United States but often failed because American managers tried to implement quality circles before implementing SPC. The Japanese first implemented SPC and by its nature changed the social order of work organizations, then they implemented quality circles.

Quality circles only work with reliable methodology and feedback, like that provided by SPC. Used alone, quality circles will not change a system. First, the system has to change; then the tools will be effective. This is why I expressed pessimism about the sporting goods retailer that wanted to implement TQM. In my opinion, they had not changed their system, but simply wanted to implement a technique.

TQM, as well as specific quality-improvement techniques like SPC, demand the same type of training that speed does, namely the need for cross-trained employees. John F. Krafcik, a consultant to MIT's International Motor Vehicle Program says, "Around the world, there is a very strong correlation in durable goods manufacturing between quality and productivity and the use of multiskilling, worker teams and just-in-time."[18]

Inventory

Just-in-time (JIT) is one of the hottest new methods for reducing inventory. It is a center of discussion in many board rooms and on many shop floors. It improves inventory control and dramatically reduces inventory overhead by restructuring an organization so operational employees have greater authority and responsibility.

JIT is often referred to as a "pull" system. This is in contrast to the normal material-movement system, which "pushes" material through a production area. Each work station pushes material from one work station to the next. In a pull system, the end user (internal customer) pulls work through the system.

A comic example of a push system was seen in an old "I Love Lucy" show. In one of these shows, Lucy is in front of a conveyor as chocolate bonbons are moving down the conveyor. Everything is all right until the line starts to move too fast. Lucy ends up stuffing bonbons in her pockets, in her dress, and in her mouth in an effort to keep up with the line. In the show, the audience breaks into laughter as the situation becomes more and more ridiculous.

In the push system, someone or something upstream has control of the flow. Most push systems are not very funny. In truth, many are even more hectic than in the comedy show because the maker and user are out of touch. Bottlenecks and backlogs are bound to occur. The only way the conveyor Lucy used could have been converted to a pull system was if Lucy had control over the flow of bonbons. Not nearly as funny, but a lot more efficient.

In theory, a pull system sounds simple enough, but it is not simple. It is very difficult to set up a pull system where the user is in control. Peter Drucker emphasizes that to implement JIT the plant must be redesigned from the end backwards and managed as an integrated flow."[19] The whole production system must be redesigned and managers must learn to think systematically about the entire production process. It is difficult but well worth the effort. When implemented, JIT dramatically reduces raw materials, work-in-process, and finished goods inventories. To achieve these savings, management must not only redesign the work area, but also the work relationships.

To implement JIT, operational employees must be given more authority including the authority to stop the production process when a problem occurs. At places like General Electric (G.E.), Harley-Davidson, and John Deere, stopping the line is a routine part of the JIT process. As the name implies, JIT consists of material, inventory, and information arriving just in time to be used. There is no safety stock; no buffer for poor decisions. It requires more accurate and exacting inventory management. Managerial ability must not only be better, but also involve everyone in the process.

Inventory control under JIT is a lot like quality control under TQM. It is everyone's responsibility, but delegating responsibility is not enough. Everyone must be trained to manage, to recognize problems, and to solve them. Like TQM, JIT changes social relationships. Delegation is not a choice; it is a necessity.

TQM, JIT, and other creative approaches are in sharp contrast to the way things used to be done. American mass-production management built on scientific management taught by Frederick Taylor and methods study developed by Frank and Lillian Gilbreth divided work into narrow, easy-to-perform tasks. Separating management and employee functions, strict divisions of labor, and narrow spans of control were accepted practices.

Much can be learned from the rationalizing of work. But increasingly, organizations are finding the old ways of doing work unacceptable in the twenty-first-century world. Newer approaches recognize the necessity of increasing variety, communication, meaning, and, most importantly, responsibility and authority in jobs. TQM/JIT operators must be cross-trained so they know several jobs in order to be able to move wherever needed. Restrictive work rules must be relaxed and competencies must be developed throughout the companies.

Concluding Thoughts

Speed, quality, and inventory management are interrelated. When you improve one area, the others also tend to improve. One other variable is related to these three and that is our trust in the ability and interests of operational people to do their jobs better.

Tell-and-sell management techniques are rapidly becoming out of date in a world that needs maximum effort from everyone. Doubtless all of us have heard this before, but never has the need been so urgent. It sometimes takes a crisis to change attitudes. The "oil war" in Kuwait changed attitudes, at least for a short while. We already knew we were oil-dependent, just as many knew we were weak competitively.

The oil situation was critical long before the Middle East crises of 1990, and may remain critical long after it. As of 1989, we imported more than 50 percent of the oil we used. We are running out of oil. At best we only have thirty years of reserves left. Oil production in the lower forty-eight states was the lowest since 1946 before the oil crisis. Still, we have not conserved; we have not looked for alternatives.

Like the oil crisis, we have a competitiveness crisis, and we have had it for some time. It has become so serious that we have lost not only jobs, but whole industries. Rather than patch up old systems, we need to redesign. There are strong pressures that are trying to flatten traditional pyramids, but there is also resistance to these changes. Marketing, product designers, and production people are often comfortable with the walls they build around themselves. Highly specialized people suffer from tunnel vision. Some upper management people want status, power, pay, and position over others. They like it the old way. Nevertheless, change will come, and those who do not change will not be around for very long.

Like the oil crisis, problems in competitiveness have been brewing for a long time. The military hierarchical organization model has really not been working for some time. Problems are multidisciplinary; we need peer-group problem solving and workers with responsibility and experience in many areas. It has taken the Japanese and the Germans to highlight for us the value of teamwork and techniques like TQM, JIT, and SPC.

Hierarchies of power, pay, and privilege seem to fly in the face of our current needs. We need speed, world-class quality, and customer satisfaction. We need globally competitive organizations that reduce overhead and maximize resources. Our greatest resource is our people, and our best way to maximize that resource is to set up a system where this is possible—a horizontal management system.

Notes

1. "Well-Run Companies: The Secret of Success," *U.S. News and World Report*, Oct. 10 1983, p. 74.

2. Tom Peters, "Flatten Pyramid Organizations for Success in the '90s," *Springfield News Leader*, 16 July 1990, p. 1.

3. Peter F. Drucker, "The Emerging Theory of Manufacturing," *Harvard Business Review*, May–June 1990, p. 98.

4. Brian Dumaine, "How Managers Can Succeed Through Speed," *Fortune,* 13 February 1989, p. 54.

5. Norm Alster, "What Flexible Workers Can Do," *Fortune,* 13 February 1989, p. 63.

6. Ibid., p. 63.

7. Neil Martin, "A Conversation with the CEO," *Fortune 1988 Investor's Guide,* p. 81.

8. Ibid., p. 61.

9. Ibid., p. 61.

10. Dumain, p. 54.

11. N. R. Kleinfield, "How Strykeforce Beat the Clock," *New York Times,* 25 March 1990, sect. 3, p. 1.

12. Dumain, p. 54.

13. Kleinfield.

14. Peters, "Flatten Pyramid Organizations.

15. "Fall Conference Unites Employee Involvement Leaders," *Teamwork* 8, no. 1 (Spring 1990), p. 2.

16. "Total Quality: Merging the Whys with the Hows," *Review,* October 1989, p. 4.

17. Peter F. Drucker, "The Emerging Theory of Management," *Harvard Business Review,* May–June 1990, p. 95.

18. Alster, p. 63.

19. Drucker, "Emerging Theory," p. 100.

Part II
Serving the Customer

3
Horizontal Management: The Structure

The first time I thought of the concept of horizontal management was while reading a speech given by George Fisher, the CEO of Motorola, Inc., to the Stanford Manufacturing Conference. In his talk he discussed American industries' increasing competitiveness due to a back-to-basics approach that has centered on rediscovering the customer. He emphasized that our competitiveness rests on our ability to make the customer the focus of corporate strategy.

He went on to make the point that the traditional organization focuses a manager's attention on the people above and below him or her on the organizational chart. He wondered where the customer and supplier fit in. His main line of thought was that it takes a horizontal organization to serve the customer.[1] This includes finding out what the customers want, working closely with vendors, and designing products and services that meet the customer's needs.

When you begin to think about it, you realize that this production process truly does move horizontally across various departmental lines and functional responsibilities. Fisher said a horizontal approach would enhance competitiveness because the customers would more likely get what they wanted or needed. Specifically, a horizontal focus would concentrate management's attention on areas sorely needing improvement, namely manufacturing.

Many have said that American industry has paid far too much attention to finance and marketing while almost completely ignoring manufacturing. The common analogy is of a two-legged stool; all three legs are needed for stability and usefulness.

Participative Management

Fisher is far from alone in his desire to rethink our relationships within the organization. In an article in the *Harvard Business Review*, Peter Drucker said the business organization of the nineties would be less like today's model and more like a hospital, a university, or even a symphony orchestra. Drucker visualized that "employees in the new information-based company will know what they have to do without a flock of vice-presidents feeding them information and orders. One conductor, the chief executive, will be enough to keep the oboes and cellos on the same beat."[2] What he describes is still a vertical organization, but a very flat one; one with only two levels, one conductor and the rest equal partners creating a symphony of actions.

Despite its fanciful appearance, the concept is really not that revolutionary. There is today an almost continuous effort in corporate America to reevaluate organizational lines of communication and authority. It seems everyone is trying to reduce the bureaucracy and the number of managerial levels between the CEO and operational-level personnel. Typical of this approach is the current trend at DuPont. H. Gordon Smyth, the senior vice-president of DuPont's Employee Relations Department, noted that the major *evolutionary* trend in his company was the streamlining of operations by increasing the span of control. For example, he noted that DuPont had twenty fewer vice-president slots in 1987 compared to 1984. He also emphasized that many of their plants have reduced the levels of management from seven to four. The purpose was to broaden the span of control and delegate decision making downward. The result was that the quality of decisions has improved because decision making is closer to the action.[3] Delegating decision making down to the lowest level is the essence of participative management.

If you listen to top officials like Mr. Smyth and read the literature, it is clear that participative management is finally in vogue, despite the fact that it has been around since the 1920s. The surprise is that it took so long to catch on. Management experts have long known it can have some impressive advantages, including:

- greater understanding and acceptance of decisions by subordinates
- greater commitment to implementing decisions
- greater understanding of objectives
- greater fulfillment of psychological needs and, therefore, greater satisfaction
- greater team identity, cooperation, and coordination
- better means of constructive conflict resolution
- better decisions[4]

Despite obvious advantages of participative management and its counterpart, employee involvement, the concept was given serious consideration only by academic's not practitioners. Upper management sometimes paid lip service to it, usually in the form of speeches; however, middle or lower management did not even do that. Apparently, it takes a good crisis to force change.

What's in a Structure?

Earlier, I mentioned Thomas J. Watson's assertion that employees need to feel totally involved in a company's programs if they are to be effective. This is certainly true of participative management. Yet, participative management can only be effective if the *structure* exists to support it. A good organizational structure will ensure that everyone is informed about expectations and other work-related activities. If participation is built into the organization, there will naturally be open discussion and, most importantly, life-giving communication throughout the organization.

How do you build such a structure? One thing is for sure; you do not build it like you would a high-rise building with layer upon layer. There are many companies though that do exactly that. The higher one rises in such a company, the farther away one is from the "ground floor" of company operations. How can you possibly have effective communication and participation when multiple *levels* of perks, power and positions, and pay still exist?

It is impossible to be truly effective at communicating, let alone at empowering people, as long as there are vertical levels within an organization. Ideas and directives flow downstream easily, but upstream only with tremendous effort. When one member of a company exerts force, power, and position over another, it alters the way that second individual does or does not respond. Colleagues and friends can freely communicate thoughts, perceptions, and values, but a boss organizes, controls, directs, and manages.

Even a benevolent boss is still a boss. No matter how you stack it, when you are a subordinate you belong to (look it up in the dictionary) an inferior or lower order. To one degree or another you are considered minor, insignificant, subnormal, unequal. Even in an orchestra, someone will "play second fiddle." In the typical vertical organization, you are a servant who works for another in return for a salary. The higher in the pecking order, the higher the salary.

I think many organizational managers recognize intuitively the innate inequity of most work, where many insignificants toil to provide power and money to the critical few. To that end, many have made changes, even if they are minor changes, in work arrangements. Often these have had dramatic results. Corporate staffs are shrinking everywhere. In fact, large corporate staffs are gradually becoming outdated, even obsolete. In large part this change is due to the explosion of information and computer technology. Thanks to powerful information technology, a few can monitor a vast number. Jewell Westerman, a consultant in organizational issues, said that some of his clients have gone from a dozen layers of management between the chief executive and front line supervisors to six, and he thinks maybe one more level could go.[5]

What's in a Title?

One more level might go and still maintain the traditional, although more streamlined, more empowered, decision-making organization. While many companies are trying to develop a more horizontal organization by shortening lines of authority, others are making changes in working relationships in the hope of obtaining greater employee involvement. One example is the proliferation of the "associate."

We have gone from "subordinate" to neutral concepts like "personnel" to one of the newer terms, "associate." Many of our better-run organizations, like Wal-Mart, have engrained the concept into their corporate language. The associate concept does represent a significant departure from the traditional master-servant relationship. There is less stigma of inferiority provided the title is more than CEO rhetoric. In more progressive companies such as Wal-Mart, the associate is truly seen as a companion, a partner, or a colleague. With this status increase, associates have at least partial membership in the institution in order to jointly pursue a common cause. Perhaps the next transformation will be for members of companies to identify each other, as George Fisher says, as (internal) consumers/suppliers.

In the best cases today, employees (associates) are being given greater authority, responsibility, and autonomy. Such actions can be a powerful tool in increasing competitiveness. Continuous success is built in incremental improvements, and only an engaged work force can do that.

Tall and Fat

Few would dispute the conclusion that flat pyramids are a better organizational structure than tall pyramids. Certainly, they are better than the diamond-shaped organizational structures seen in many real-life companies (see figure 3–1). Although there have been efforts in this direction, there are still far too many organizations bloated with excessive numbers of middle management personnel.

But even these portly pyramids are better than inverted pyramids (see figure 3–2). Unfortunately, there are plenty of these around as well. Mi-

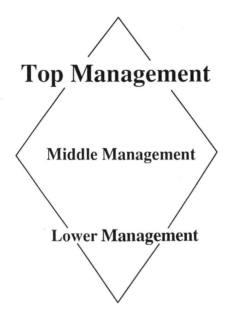

Figure 3–1. Diamond-shaped Organizational Structure

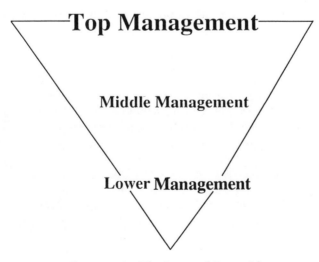

Figure 3–2. The Inverted Pyramid

chael L. Tennican, a director at Temple, Barker, and Sloane, Inc., notes that these inverted pyramids are not uncommon in offices. He said that his firm survey of two hundred representatives shows that from World War II to the mid-1960s companies resembled pyramids, with four of every five employees working on the assembly line or some other production job. Tennican says the pyramid has been turned on its head. There are now four managers or supervisors for every production worker.[6]

He goes on to say that diversification has given rise to this bureaucracy as corporate headquarters add more staff to supply the expertise that does not exist at lower levels. Regardless of the causes, it is to corporate America's credit that many have begun to trim excess staff and nonoperational personnel. Flat is in. How flat an organization can evolve is anyone's guess, but it is clear that the metamorphosis has begun.

Flat and Focused

Our discussion of a need for more horizontal organizations began with the current concern over and recognition of the importance of customer satisfaction. George Fisher of Motorola made this point abundantly clear. In a search to demonstrate a greater resolve and greater commitment to the customer, some have talked about "total customer satisfaction." However, "total customer satisfaction" will not and cannot occur until companies implement more horizontal organization.

Companies like Motorola, Hewlett-Packard, and Wal-Mart have been able to increase customer satisfaction by focusing on an almost obsessive concern for the customer's viewpoint. World-class companies like Motorola, Federal Express, and Metropolitan Life Insurance Company (Met Life) have slowly transformed themselves into organizations with a horizontal management style. For example, with over 70,000 employees, Federal Express only has five levels between the CEO and operational levels. Still, it takes more than flat pyramids to create a horizontal management style; it also takes a refocusing of management's attention.

The traditional vertical and horizontal styles differ from each other not so much in the number of levels of organization, although fewer levels certainly make it easier to implement a horizontal perspective. Instead, it is the focus of the communication that is the key difference. Fisher notes, a traditional organizational chart focuses your attention on people above and below you and he wonders, "Where do customers and suppliers fit in?"[7] He believes a horizontal organization is needed to truly serve customers. It is only in this way that we can find out what customers want and then develop close coordination between vendors, designers, and production to produce products and services that are of the highest quality at the lowest cost, which can then be delivered quickly to customers.

A horizontal approach is not an option; it is a requirement because it focuses management's efforts on the true function of business, namely to serve the customer. Hollis L. Harris, president and CEO for Delta Air Lines, expressed it best when he said, "If you take care of customers, the profits will take care of themselves."[8]

NOAC

At the moment no institution can be called a pure horizontal-management organization, but many are rapidly transforming themselves through a variety of ways. One of the most powerful ways to make vertical organizations horizontal is called Next Operation As Customer (NOAC). Motorola, Met Life, and a host of other organizations use this technique by making a point of identifying each department and each individual within the organization as an internal customer or supplier. That is the key point of NOAC—customers or suppliers can be either internal or external. The central concept of NOAC is that information flows between customers and suppliers outside and within the organization. While there may be only one external customer, every department, every individual has internal customers and suppliers within the organization.

Identifying one's external customers is usually fairly easy, but isolating one's internal customers and suppliers takes much more thought. For instance, an office manager may be one of Purchasing's customers, for Purchasing provides the office manager with office supplies. If, for example, Production Control requests Purchasing to procure specific materials for them, Production Control has supplied the request to Purchasing, which is now the customer. These relationships are quite fluid, for when Purchasing fills Production Control's request, it is a supplier again (see figure 3–3).

As can be seen, it is not always easy to identify specific internal customer and supplier relationships, but it is necessary if one is to improve customer service and competitiveness. Managers adopting a horizontal approach can begin by having everyone within the organization determine their suppliers and customers. As seen in figure 3–3, these relationships are often circular. When providing information or products, you are a supplier. When you receive those requests, you are the customer.

In this manner, everyone identifies their suppliers and customers. From a NOAC perspective the production process begins when an external customer interacts with others (usually the salesperson), and concludes by working backward through the various series of internal suppliers and customers. The customer transaction concludes when it comes full circle and the customer (theoretically) receives what he or she wanted.

Identifying these *communication links* within the organization is critical to implementing horizontal management within a vertical organiza-

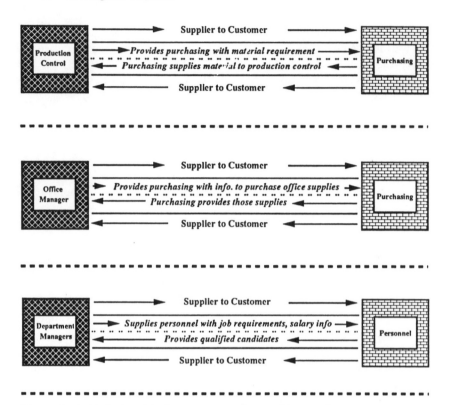

Figure 3–3. Relationship between supplier and internal customers can be a two-way street.

tion. One way to do this is to use a visual graph similar to a sociogram. A sociogram shows social preferences within a group, thereby identifying overchosen members (those frequently chosen) and isolates. A similar graph, a "structure graph," could be created to identify internal customers and suppliers.

Such a "structure graph" will probably reveal a network of communication links similar to the one for the personnel department seen in figure 3–4. The graph in figure 3–4 shows arrows going back and forth between departments. These represent supplier/customer interactions. In very complex networks, it might be necessary to graph supplier/customer networks separately. For a white-collar process or department, there may be several internal customers, as in figure 3–4. In this example, the personnel department often serves both as customer and supplier to the same departments. In the example given, the personnel department supplies applicants with information while also requiring other information. The same could be said of the relationship between personnel and production control, purchasing, and the office manager. At one time or another, each

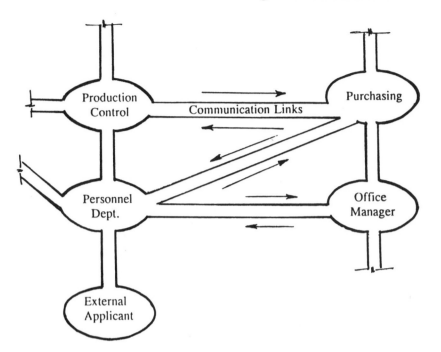

Figure 3–4. Partial Network of Communication Links

one of these will need to act as a supplier or customer to the personnel department. In order to avoid "paralysis through analysis," only the most important customers should be considered a top priority.

Once these relationships are identified, you can begin to assess how to improve the speed and quality of the relationships. (In the next chapter we will see how such an assessment can help each individual and each area understand both where they fit in and how they affect the operation of the organization.) This entails defining measurable characteristics, assessing performance, determining weaknesses, and drawing up corrective strategies. All corrective strategies must begin with the NOAC golden rule: If *any* internal customer requirements are in conflict with the organization's final external customer, the external customer's needs take priority. External customer needs should supersede all internal relationships within the organization if horizontal management is to be used as a competitive tool to increase customer satisfaction.

Fibers and Networks

Horizontal management can best be visualized by thinking of each communication link as a conduit analogous to an optical fiber. You can think

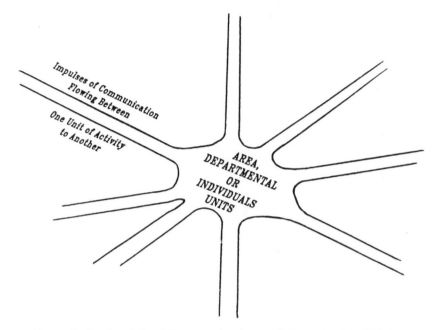

Figure 3–5. Conduit of Communication and Organizational Units

of each fiber or strand of this organizational network as representing a series of transactions or impulses between internal customers and suppliers (see figure 3–5).

The purpose of managers on these conduits of communication fibers is to ensure the satisfaction of the customer's or adjacent work cell's needs and requirements. Impulses that travel back and forth through this conduit are the various requests, memos, reports, and analyses needed to conduct business. These messages are transmitted through various units until they reach the end unit where the initial customer request is acted upon.

At this point, the ending departmental or individual receiving unit begins to satisfy the customer's (or previous unit's) needs. This process then moves back through the various units of the network until it reaches the originating or external customer.

For instance, assume an external customer applies for insurance. In this case, the sales representative (or unit) provides the customer with information about the product. Assume the sales representative then submits the completed application to the branch office. It is then transmitted to a branch office's quality business clerk. The policy application then goes to an underwriter who approves or disapproves it. If the application is approved, it starts back through the customer communication conduit. First, it is sent to the issue clerk, then to the branch administrator, next to the sales representative, and finally to the external customer.

APPLICANT/POLICYHOLDER

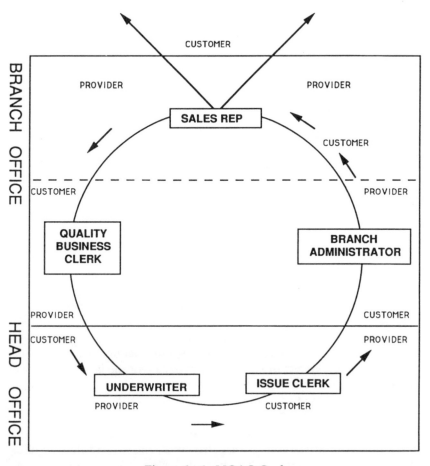

Figure 3–6. NOAC Cycle

As the application begins to proceed laterally through the various department units, the sales representative becomes the first internal supplier (see figure 3–6). As such, the sales representative provides his or her internal customer (quality business clerk) with the correct paperwork and related impulse information. This completes the originating customer's request. As underwriting issues the policy and moves forward through the departmental units, the supplier/customer relationship is reversed.

Kinks and Fractures

This vision of how to design and run an organization is obviously different from the structure of the typical vertical organization. Unless one were to have the good fortune to be working with a completely horizontal organization, this network of transmitting and receiving impulses from internal suppliers and customers will occur within the vertical organization where communication moves up and down—mostly down. Despite the continuous drive toward "flat organizations" with fewer managerial levels between the CEO and operational personnel, the problem with communication breakdown remains. In fact, in a survey of the causes of poor productivity and quality, industrial engineers gave their strongest response to the issue of communication and cooperation between departments. An emphatic 88 percent said they *strongly agree* that the lack of communication and cooperation between different components of business leads to reduced productivity.[9]

Concluding Thoughts

Until an organization is completely horizontal, the hierarchial levels of management remain the primary focus of organizational communication. Horizontal communication focuses on the customer rather than the hierarchy.

Vertical organizations are designed to move communication up and down through the organization. In reality, information also moves sideways. Without a system or structure to take care of the lateral transfer of information, the organization loses effectiveness. We could say it begins to splinter, fracture, and develop kinks in the organizational communication conduit.

The communication breakdowns come in all shapes and sizes. One thing they have in common is that they affect the smooth flow of informational impulses. Some of these breakdowns can rupture and tangle the flow to the point that the organizational system breaks down. The result is lost sales, lost customers, and lost profits.

Communication breakdowns can also build in unnecessary overhead. Communication kinks and loops cause errors, backtracking, lost time and effort processing or checking for defects, and higher costs. As such, these kinks and loops affect the smooth flow of information, services, and products between the external and internal customers and their suppliers. The result is failure to meet customer expectations.

Organizations with the fewest kinks, loops, and fractures in transmission are the ones that best serve the customer. A series of customer/supplier transactions without communication problems is the same thing as DOING IT RIGHT THE FIRST TIME.

Horizontally structured organizations have less chance of developing transmission and reception problems because lines of communication are simpler, more direct, and shorter. However, as we shall see, a flatter organization with NOAC links identified is not the total answer. Smooth customer/supplier transactions and error-free communication will only occur in a totally flat or completely horizontal organization. That is what this book is about.

Notes

1. George Fisher, "Our Time Has Come: A Manufacturing Renaissance," *Executive Speeches*, Dayton, Ohio The Executive Speaker® Company October 1988, p. 8.
2. Jeremy Main, "The Winning Organization," *Fortune*, 26 September 1988, p. 50.
3. Gordon H. Smyth, Remarks to Employee Relations Department at North Carolina A & T, 11 February 1987, pp. 4–5.
4. G. A. Yukl, *Leadership in Organizations*, (Englewood Cliffs, N.J.: Prentice-Hall, 1981), p. 208.
5. Main, p. 52.
6. David G. Wallace, Dean Foust, Teri Thompson, and others, "America's Leanest and Meanest," *Business Week*, 5 October 1987, p. 81.
7. Fisher, p. 8.
8. Hollis L. Harris, "Recapturing a Singleness of Purpose," *Air Transport World Conference*, Washington, D.C., 4 October 1988, p. 6.
9. "Productivity and Quality Survey," *Focus: Industrial Engineering*, April 1990, p. 6.

4
NOAC: Tracking Communication Flow

Assessing the quality of work and setting standards of performance are essential to the success of any enterprise, including implementing horizontal management. One way to do this is to answer a series of questions designed to assist in problem-identification. (A summary of these questions is included in table 4–1.) The first one of these questions is "What do I do?" It is also necessary to identify what activities, products, and services others must provide for you before you can do your job. From a horizontal management perspective the question to ask is, "What do I need from my suppliers?" and "Why do I need it?"

Next, identify your customer or those to whom you supply goods and service. Focus on only the most important ones as a first priority. Only when you have identified your major internal customers can you begin to assess their requirements and needs. Each particular department or individual may do several things, but only the most important functions should be examined. In identifying the functions or services that you provide for your customers, it is wise to focus on those customer services you provide that can be observed and measured. Next, write down each task associated with each function. For example, if you have been requested to conduct a study (by another manager), what tasks might be involved? Once you have a list of those tasks needed to complete the job, ask yourself questions similar to those suggested by Jo An Loop.[1] These questions are in table 4–2.

Once an important and tangible service has been identified, then select and evaluate a step or service that has the greatest potential for improvement. Likely candidates might be those that would result in the greatest improvement in quality, cost, reduction in cycle time, or some other high-priority issue, but only the customer can make this determination. Sometimes the answer is obvious. At other times, it may require some investigation. Having chosen an area that you feel is important to the customer, determine the customer's requirements.

At this point, you are finally ready to measure and evaluate performance. The customer determines measurement criteria and the perfor-

Table 4–1
The NOAC Road Map

Step	Comments
1. DETERMINE FINAL CUSTOMER & HIS REQUIREMENTS	This is, generally, the external customer. Internal customer requirements may be in conflict with the final, external customer. The latter's requirements are paramount.
2. FLOW CHART THE PROCESS	Products, information, paper move horizontally across organizational charts.
3. DETERMINE THE MAJOR INTERNAL CUSTOMERS IN EACH PROCESS STEP	For a white-collar process or department, there may be several customers. Only the most important customers should be considered as a first priority.
4. DETERMINE THE MAJOR FUNCTIONS/ SERVICES IN EACH PROCESS STEP	A particular process or department may have several functions. Only the most important functions should be examined. (These functions or services should be tangible–visible to a 3rd party.)
5. SELECT THE PROCESS STEP WITH GREATEST IMPROVEMENT POTENTIAL	This is based on the step with the largest quality problem (external customer viewpoint), or the largest cost or longest cycle time.
6. DETERMINE MAIN CUSTOMER REQUIREMENTS	These are specifications—from internal customer to "process owner" of the process step and from process owner to supplier of the process.
7. DETERMINE MEASURES OF EFFECTIVENESS	Measurement criteria and scores must be determined by the customer, but must be agreed to by the process owner or department head as fair and meaningful to both sides. Typical general criteria in support services are: timeliness, accuracy, completeness, cooperativeness, etc.

Table 4–1 continued

Step	Comments
8. DETERMINE CAUSE OF VARIANCE (GAP) FROM REQUIREMENTS	Examples of causes: poor output specs; poor input specs; lack of consequences to organization and/or individual for not performing to requirements; lack of feedback; poor process itself; inadequate resources.
9. IMPROVE PROCESS STEP	See improvement tools.
10. REPEAT STEPS 5–9 ON NEXT PROCESS STEP	Select the next process step with the 2nd greatest potential for quality, cost, cycle time improvement.

Source: Motorola, Inc. (by permission).

Table 4–2
The NOAC Checklist

You now have a list of tasks for your department, you have identified your supplier and customer, and the required input and output. For each of your activities now ask yourself the following questions:

1. Does performing this activity add value?

2. What are management's requirements for this activity?

3. What are my requirements for this activity?

4. Are the requirements documented?

5. What would be the impact if this activity were eliminated?

6. What processes are required to meet the requirements?

7. Does my current activity conform to requirements?

8. What might keep me from doing this activity right the first time?

9. What should be measured to assure conformance to requirements?

Table 4–2 continued

10. How can the activity be simplified?

11. Could the activity meet my customer's requirements and expectations?

List the answers to these questions on a separate sheet of paper, and discuss them with your manager or supervisor. The answers to these questions will give both of you a greater understanding of the activity itself, and may also be used as a guide to developing written documentation of its requirements.

Source: 31st Annual APICS International Conference Proceedings, 1988.

mance evaluation but both supplier and customer must agree the measurement is fair and meaningful. Sometimes a supervisor is needed to insure that supplier and customer reach an acceptable agreement. The criteria to be evaluated change with the situation, but it usually revolves around a supplier's accuracy, thoroughness, cooperativeness, reliability, availability, or other relevant measure.

Once internal customers evaluate the service and products of their suppliers, areas needing improvement can be identified. The difference between what was expected and what was achieved is the performance gap. The key question the supplier must answer is "What do I need to do a better job (in the customer's eyes)?" A variety of assessment tools can be used to answer this question. In a moment we will look at how Met Life used a highly flexible way to assess their performance.

When a performance gap is identified, the supplier determines the cause and corrects it. These causes can include (1) poor customer specifications, (2) lack of consequences to the organization for failure to meet expectations, (3) lack of feedback, (4) use of a poor production process, and (5) inadequate resources or other causes.

Met Life's NOAC

This brings up an important point. Any organization that is seriously considering implementing a NOAC perspective must be willing to teach those within the organization how to solve customer/supplier problems. Companies that have had success implementing NOAC concepts made training a key part of their process. Met Life called their customer service activities the Quality Improvement Process (QIP). It was introduced in the organization in 1985 through a corporate-wide program that trained key personnel in quality concepts.

When Met Life began QIP in late 1985 and early 1986, their corporate quality personnel and trainers developed the corporate training program. Each department within the corporation selected a few individuals to deliver the corporate training program to supervisory and management personnel. The training, which took about three months, emphasized a variety of problem-solving, communication, participation, and quality-awareness techniques. Corporate training materials included handout exercises, visual aids, and video tapes.

Setting Up Horizontal Networks in a Pyramid

Once the training was complete, Met Life conducted *identification meetings* to identify the major products and services for each department and the customers. In essence, they were identifying the conduits of customer transactions. Next, each department's customers were identified, and a "product champion" was chosen for each customer transaction. These champions were individually responsible for quality and application of QIP for a particular product or service. Met Life then built up a "quality network" around each of these customer transactions. This involved branch, regional, and corporate quality officers who were responsible for setting parameters and evaluating results.

As originally envisioned, these networks, as seen in figure 4–1, consisted of Quality Improvement Teams (QIT), which were drawn from employee Natural Work Teams. QITs concentrated on identifying and solving problems that involved customer and quality issues such as unnecessary recycling of work, poor work processes, and multiple handling of work. The objective was to "Do things right the first time," rather than to recycle work over and over again. Anything less meant more work, extra processing of information, lower accuracy and productivity, and a longer response time.

From the beginning of their efforts, Met Life always wanted to integrate quality into their management process. To insure this, they developed an objective-setting process and monitored it by a corporate reporting system that tracks performance against objectives. They also established a training program and other activities to support their structures.

Today, the customer-service networks at Met Life concentrate on improving the performance and service standards and reducing extra inspection, rework, errors, and other shortcomings. An example of this approach is seen in figure 4–2. Met Life defines the knots and kinks in their communication links as Extra Processing (EP). This is waste within their production system. As new work, claims, proposals, complaints, and so forth flow into an area, they are processed. Value is added to the product or service as the work moves from one area to the next. At any point, EP or

EXHIBIT 1   # WORK RELATIONSHIPS

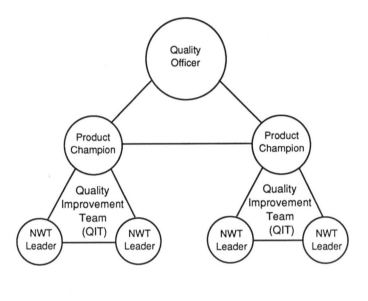

Natural Work Teams
(NWT)

Figure 4–1. The Quality Improvement Process Network

Courtesy of Metropolitan Life

kinks in their system can become a problem. If information is handled more than it needs to be, it is EP. If errors are made, it is EP. Excessive inspecting, double checking, and verification are all forms of EP. Obviously, EP can be time consuming and very costly and is something that should be eliminated.

Met Life kept their vertical organization, but implanted these horizontal communication networks in their system. The result was an opened communication line and improving decision making. John J. Falzon, senior vice-president of Quality and Planning at Met Life, noted that "over time many departments adjusted their formal organization to work more effectively with their QIP network teams and some even reorganized to conform to the network."[2]

While employee participation was improved through Met Life's horizontal network of QIP teams, the primary purpose of the QIP team system was to identify customer-service problems. This can be restated as the

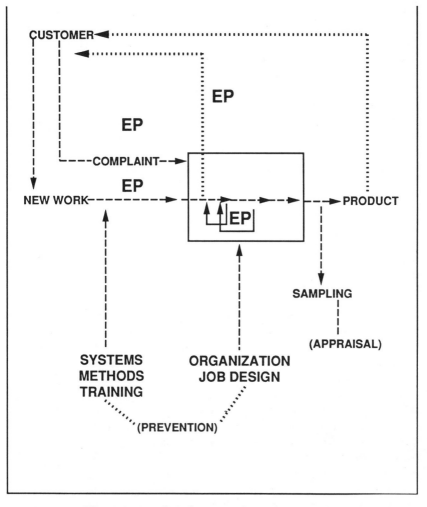

Figure 4–2. Identification of Extra Processing

questions, "How do we find out what the customer desires and once we know, how do we assess our performance so it can be improved?" To answer these questions, Met Life relied heavily on the work of three Texas A & M researchers, Valerie Zeithmal, Parasuram and Leonard Berry.[3]

Standards

Standards in manufacturing are fairly easy to establish. Either the product performs to specifications or it does not. Either it is usable or it is not. It works or it does not. Quality measures are difficult to develop in service, office, and white-collar work, especially in nonproduction and nonrepetitive activities. Services are also intangible and sometimes difficult to verify because it is hard to separate the evaluation of a service from opinion about those who provide the service. Nevertheless, it is essential to NOAC specifically and, in general, to horizontal management that measures must be established that accurately reflect customer needs in all important areas, not simply in those areas that are easy to measure.

This was the problem facing Met Life and this is where the research by Texas A & M professors Parasuram, Zeithmal, and Berry helped. These researchers showed that individuals are critical to the quality of service and that often how customers are treated is as important as the service they receive.

Service Dimensions

The Texas A & M researchers addressed the problem of measuring service by first measuring the difference between what customers expected to receive and what they felt they actually received.[4] The difference between customer expectation and perception is the size of the service problem. The researchers were able to identify five factors that influenced customers' overall evaluation of service quality. These five dimensions of service are a supplier's responsiveness, reliability, assurance, and empathy, as well as the tangible results of the service work.

With these dimensions as a starting point, Met began measuring the difference between customer expectations and perception on each dimension. John J. Falzon, vice-president of Quality and Planning at Met Life notes, "The difference between the customer expectation level on each dimension and how the customer perceives a company's delivery of that dimension is quantifiable, measurable, and can be expressed as a 'gap' in service quality."[5] A critical point is that by measuring these variables you can develop a series of measures that can be evaluated and traced over a period of time.

Met Life expects its departments to develop appropriate survey instruments. One example of such a survey was developed by Met Life's Policy Issue Team. The team wanted to eliminate EP and improve services to their internal customers. John J. Falzon noted that in 1987, the Policy Issue Team first developed a questionnaire that included the five service dimensions including the need for responsiveness. Two examples of statements concerning responsiveness were "Calling Underwriting will not usually speed my case" and "Electronic mail may get faster action than the phone."

When the questionnaire was administered, it showed several gaps between internal customers' expectations and what they perceived they had received. The Policy Improvement Team attacked this problem in a variety of ways to improve customer perception of the services being delivered. John J. Falzon noted that the sales office used to use electronic mail for inquiries about the status of their cases. These customers then followed up with telephone calls about the cases. This double inspection is an example of EP or communication kinks referred to earlier. After some investigation, the team found that the telephone calls were made because sales personnel were not receiving acknowledgments of the electronic mail messages. A simple acknowledgment now lets sales people know the status of their cases: this has resulted in fewer telephone calls and a decrease in EP.

The process of identifying these performance gaps was fairly simple. If, for example, a respondent indicates a "7" response on one of the *expectation* questions, then the customer has assigned a high value to that particular item. For example, if a customer circles a "7" when the question refers to dealing with business matters in a confidential manner, then the customer is saying he or she assigns great importance to confidentiality. On the other hand, if the same customer indicates only a "2" rating on the *perception* scale about confidentiality, then there is a gap of 5. Thus, a supplier can actually get a reading on the degree that they are or are not meeting customer expectations. The greater the gap, the larger the problem. This way it is possible to quantify customer service so that specific problems can be pinpointed.

According to John J. Falzon, the gap between customer perceptions and expectations can occur when management does not understand customer expectations. He said it can also occur if management does understand customer expectations, but does not set service standards that reflect that understanding. Even if management understands customer expectations and sets good standards, a gap can occur if the delivery of services does not live up to standards. Poor communication can also cause gaps when management or marketing raises expectations that cannot be met.

As in Met Life's case, once you have an idea of what your internal or external customers think of you, it is wise to benchmark your competition. You need to compare your external customers' opinions of both your organization and your competition. The lower your ranking compared to your competition, the more serious and urgent the problem.

Management's Role

NOAC consists of networks of transactions. Often these layers, or networks, may become tangled and dysfunctional because more than one person or department is transmitting and receiving with a variety of customers and suppliers. The greater the number of interactions, the greater the risk of developing problems.

To untangle and straighten out these problems, you need to find out, as Met Life did, where the problem is occurring. Start by tracking customer transactions through the organization. By tracking transactions backward from the external customer to the originating supplier and then forward again to delivery of the final product or service, you can isolate breakdowns and "kinks."

For instance, a manager may trace the paperwork involved in a customer transaction and discover the service is too slow. Having isolated a problem, he or she may then use a variety of problem-solving tools, such as the Cause and Effect Diagram, to identify exactly what is slowing down the process and increasing costs. (An example of this technique is seen in figure 9–4.) Referring to the insurance example in the previous chapter, a manager in this organization might discover that underwriting is doing extra processing (e.g. making errors) because they do not have enough information. Just as likely, the manager could discover that these extra processing loops and knots may be due to errors in paperwork that underwriting is receiving from their supplier. Isolating these causes can take time, but it is the only way the organization can design a system to prevent, rather than simply react to, communication problems.

Prevention of problems is always preferable to damage control. Whenever possible, it is wise to prevent kinks and communication tangles rather than to have to unravel them. Problems in the customer-transaction conduit of a corporation can be prevented through measures that include educating customers and suppliers about what can and what needs to be done. Better training of personnel, improved diagnostic tools like SPC, better customer feedback tools, greater employee involvement and motivation, and the development of closer relationships between design, production, and marketing are viable ways to prevent problems from occurring.

Even extensive use of preventive measures cannot eliminate all problems as the transaction moves from supplier to internal or external customer. Inevitably, problems will occur. While all of the above techniques work to resolve problems as well as to prevent them, it will also be necessary to establish problem-solving systems. Quality circles, problem-solving teams, and face-to-face communication techniques that make use of open-ended questioning, paraphrasing, and brainstorming all can be viable tools to track and better manage customer transactions.

Concluding Thoughts

In horizontal management, subordinate-supervisor relationships are as obsolete as the horse and buggy. Establishing NOAC relationships is one alternative, and may even serve as a transitional phase to more equitable arrangements.

Horizontal organizations are very different from vertical ones. Even very flat organizations with few layers of managers still focus on subordinate-supervisor relationships. The horizontal organization does not have lines of authority. Instead, it has networks of transactions.

Those companies that begin to develop a horizontal management system often begin by first identifying key customer transactions, then identifying the problems in the critical supplier relationships and developing solutions. However, this is only the beginning. To develop a competitive advantage is to make fundamental changes in the way business is organized.

Met Life's systematic attempt at establishing a system for implementing NOAC can provide a model for others who want to develop horizontal networks gradually while still maintaining a vertical organization. Success depends on managerial support, employee involvement, and a system for identifying, assessing, and improving the relationships between suppliers and customers. NOAC bypasses interdepartmental barriers and politics: it focuses rather on a win-win strategy with the (internal *and* external) customer at the center. That is not a bad beginning.

Notes

1. R. Jo An Loop, "Managing Quality Improvement in Support," *31st Annual APICS International Conference Proceedings*, Las Vegas, Nevada, 17–26 October 1988, pp. 287–89.

2. John J. Falzon, "A Quest for Quality: One Company's Experience," unpublished document, p. 6.

3. Valerie Zeithmal Parasuram, and Leonard L. Berry, "Servqual: A Multiple-Item Scale for Measuring Customer Perceptions of Service Quality," Report No. 86–108 (Cambridge, Mass.: Marketing Science Institute, 1986).

4. Ibid.

5. Falzon, p. 6.

5
Focus on the Customer: Bringing Outsiders Inside

NOAC and the more general concept of horizontal management are not synonymous. NOAC is just one possible way of enhancing the flow of horizontal communication within an organization. By implementing NOAC, management is often able to streamline the decision-making and communication flow.

To completely achieve a customer perspective, management must openly embrace their *external* customers by bringing them into the very decision-making process of the organization. Doing this creates a more competitive and horizontal organization, more competitive because the organization has delegated more autonomy, authority, and responsibility to the lowest operational level, allowing front-line service and product providers to respond rapidly to the customer's needs and desires, and more horizontal because employees are empowered when they feel they are an important part of the entrepreneurial spirit throughout the organization.

Two companies that have probably gone further than anyone else in translating the "voice of the customer" throughout their respective organizations are American Express and Motorola, Inc. American Express, a service company, does it through "customer-based" transactions. Motorola, a manufacturer, does it through effective product design and by incorporating the customer perspective throughout the design and production stages of manufacturing.

Customer-Based Transactions at American Express

American Express has probably taken the concept of management based on customer transactions further than anyone else. MaryAnne Rasmussen, vice-president of Worldwide Quality Assurance for American Express Travel Related Services Company, notes that American Express began to realize it was not enough to measure the work of individual departments, rather, the total customer-transaction process needed to be assessed. To that end, they began eliminating communication filters and started monitoring the communications and information flow from one end of the organization to the other. Then they segregated the credit card service into discrete customer transactions that were visible to and measurable by customers, such as billing, paying retail establishments, replacing lost or stolen cards, and so on.

Next, they developed numerous performance measures based on these individual customer transactions. For instance, some of their performance measures include timeliness in processing basic applications, in processing emergency card replacement, and in mailing card members' statements. Timeliness is not the only measure they use. Accuracy in processing card member address changes and accuracy of processing chargebacks and inquiries are other measurements. In fact they have over one hundred separate measures in their card business alone.

American Express not only measured individual customer transactions, they also restructured their business to resemble a horizontal organization. They have made use of customer-transaction surveys based on single interactions between customers and the front-line customer-service personnel. These single-transaction surveys are designed to ask each individual such things as (1) customer's opinion of the product (credit card), (2) customer's opinion of the company, (3) intention to renew, and (4) future usage plans.

According to Raymond L. Larkin, executive vice-president of Operations, Credit Control, and Quality Assurance, measuring their service performance had a profound effect on the way American Express did business. As a result of the information they got, they changed workflows, eliminated unnecessary steps, came up with new methods, procedures, and ideas, reconstructed the organization, and changed reporting lines to better serve the customer.[1]

Did all of these changes make a difference? According to MaryAnne Rasmussen, the answer is a resounding "yes." Rasmussen notes that quality of service delivery improved by 78 percent, while at the same time expenses per transaction were reduced by 21 percent. They reduced card member application processing time by 37 percent. (This one improvement saved them over $70 million in ten years.)[2]

Such improvements have not only had a positive effect on the bottom line, but also continue to have a positive effect on customer satisfaction. In 1986 the percent of card members whose expectations were exceeded improved. In 1986 the percentage was 82 percent; in 1988 it was 94 percent.

Motorola's Customer Satisfaction Process

"Total customer satisfaction" is the fundamental objective of Motorola. It might be noted that in 1988 Motorola won the United States's first quality award, the Malcolm Baldrige Award. They won in large part because they make customer satisfaction the heart of their planning process. Their customer satisfaction efforts are based on five key operational initiatives.

The first of these is what they call Six Sigma Quality. By 1992 Motorola's objective is to be at the six sigma level of quality. This is a statistical term that essentially means, "achieving a variation in performance such that defects will occur in products and services less than four times per million opportunities, or that there is a 99.999996 percent chance that no defects will occur per opportunity."[3]

With three sigma there will be 2,700 defects per million opportunities, rather than the 3.4 defects for six sigma. Mikel J. Harry, principle staff engineer for the Government Electronics group at Motorola, describes the difference in quality in terms of cleaning a 1,500 square-foot house with wall-to-wall carpeting. If the quality of the carpet, in terms of cleanliness, was at the zero sigma level then 100 percent of the carpet in the house (1,500 square feet) would be soiled. On the other hand, if the carpet were to be cleaned at the three sigma level, there would be about four square feet of carpet soiled. This would be approximately equivalent to the carpet area under the typical recliner chair. Now, if the carpet had been cleaned to the six sigma level, there would only be an area the size of a pin head still soiled.[4]

Suppose the quality changes by 1.5 sigma when it "slips a little bit." For the sake of argument, suppose the person cleaning the carpet showed up slightly intoxicated. Imagine the person staggering around trying to clean the carpet. How much of the carpet do you suppose would not get cleaned because of this? Well, let's see. If our carpet cleaner normally performed to three sigma sober, then under the condition of slight inebriation we could expect to see about 100 square feet of soiled carpet when the job was finished. This would be an area about the size of a second bedroom. On the other hand, if the cleaner normally performed to six sigma (sober, that is), we could expect to see an area still soiled about the size of the bottom of the cleaner's empty shot glass.[5] Other comparisons of the differences in quality levels are seen in figure 5–1.

To do this Motorola must design products that "will accept a *reasonable* variation in component parts, and develop manufacturing processes that will produce minimum variation in the final output product."[6] It also means that they had to analyze all the services they provided, break them down into component steps, and redesign these steps so they can be performed to the six sigma standard. They use statistical measures to record the defects found in every function and relate it to the product or process that is involved.

The key point is that they use measurement as a language to focus everyone's attention on the customer and quality issue. They used a common metric called *defects per unit*, the definition of which was the same throughout the company. No more jargon here. "A defect was anything

PPM	SIGMAS	AREA*	SPELLING*	DISTANCE*
0.000003	7σ	Point of a sewing needle	1 misspelled word in all of the books contained in several large libraries	1/8 of an inch
000.002	6σ	Size of a typical diamond	1 misspelled word in all of the books contained in a small library	4 steps in any direction
0000.57	5σ	Size of the bottom of your telephone	1 misspelled word in a set of encyclopedias	A trip to the local gas station
000.063	4σ	Floor space of a typical living room	1 misspelled word per 30 pages (about one chapter in book)	45 min. of freeway driving (any direction)
002.700	3σ	Floor space of a small hardware store	15 misspelled words per page in a book	Coast-to-coast trip
045.600	2σ	Floor space of a large super-market	25 misspelled words per page in a book	1-1/2 times around the world
317.400	1σ	Floor space of an average factory	170 misspelled words per page in a book	From here to the moon

Generating constants approximated on the basis of known proportions, averages, and/or best estimates. This particular table does not correct ppm for typical sources of variation. Its sole purpose is to demonstrate "practical quality differences" in relations to "equivalent standard deviation units."

Unadjusted for typical shifts and drifts in the universal average. Such an adjustment would increase ppm from 0.002 to 3.4.

Figure 5–1. Comparisons of Various Characteristics Using the Sigma Measurement Scale

Courtesy of Motorola, Inc.

which caused customer dissatisfaction, whether specified or not. A unit was a unit of work. A unit was equipment, a circuit board assembly, a page of a technical manual, a line of software code, an hour of labor, a wire transfer of funds, or whatever output your organization produced."[7]

Other Initiatives

Motorola's other initiatives are closely related to six sigma quality. One of these is to reduce the total cycle time. Motorola refers to *cycle time* as the elapsed time from the moment a customer places an order for an existing product to the time they deliver it. To reduce the cycle time, they examine their total system, including the natural horizontal link between manufacturing and marketing activities.

Their third initiative, product and manufacturing leadership, emphasizes the need for product development and for the manufacturing disciplines to work together in an integrated world. The fourth initiative is profit improvement, which is a long-term approach that helps management commit the necessary resources to give their customers what they need. The last initiative, participation management within and cooperation between organizations, is fairly self-explanatory.

The elements common to all of these initiatives is the systematic, integrated approach to problem solving and customer satisfaction. They emphasize close links between functional areas, the need to keep the customer at the center of everything that is done, and, most importantly, to involve everyone in the process. This is a pretty good working definition of horizontal network.

Becoming a world-class competitor able to compete with the Japanese or anyone else means organizing operations around the customer. Instead of separate disjointed efforts, everyone must focus on the customer's needs. There must be a clear customer-service strategy consisting of first identifying how you can please the customer. Once the customer's needs are identified, you must then determine how you stack up against the competition. Find the company that offers the best-in-class customer service, then see how your business compares to them. Finally, it is necessary to never accept the current situation. Business should always be in the process of updating its method of measurement, making changes, and improving the production of goods or the delivery of the service.

Tools for Product and Service Design

Two of the newer and more innovative techniques of identifying how you can please the customer and how you stack up against the competition are Quality Function Development (QFD) and the Taguchi method. Since the customer is the center of a horizontal management strategy, anything that focuses on the customer is important. QFD is a major advance in assessing customers, and can be a major tool in helping us focus on the customer.

When product planning is done correctly it can lead to dramatic improvements in productivity, quality, and customer satisfaction. Motorola's success was based on commitment from management, a comprehensive design and production network, and effective management and employee training. Only when this support is in place can you begin to maximize the usefulness of QFD and Taguchi Methods.

One of these new customer-focused tools being used by Toyota, Ford, Motorola, and many other world-class competitive organizations is QFD. QFD was first introduced in Japan at the Kobe Shipyard by Mitsubishi

Heavy Industries, Ltd., in 1972. Since then, manufacturing and, to a lesser degree, services are beginning to see its potential.

The QFD assessment tools offer those wishing to implement a horizontal perspective a potent way of ingraining the "view of the customer" into the very structure of the organization. They also provide a way of comparing a business to the competition and examine how effective that business is at identifying the voice of the customer. The goal of QFD is to transmit the customer's needs, desires, and requirements into an organization's engineering, parts, process, and production measurements.

QFD reduces the risk of misinterpreting customer requirements and can help insure that marketing strategies are neither lost in the day-to-day production activities nor misinterpreted by others within the organization. Production control points, those critical points within the production system that are evaluated to determine the effectiveness of the production system, are less likely to be overlooked when the QFD process is used. QFD also has the potential to minimize design changes, thereby helping to insure that all design is being done right the first time.

QFD provides organizations with a way of transmitting the customer's requirements throughout the entire design, development, and production system. Customer requirements are first expressed in the customer's own terms. Then these requirements are put into technical language that specifically identifies what is needed. Next, QFD assigns specific responsibilities for meeting the customer's needs to specific departments and sections within an organization.

QFD Matrices

The *Planning Matrix* is one of four key documents used in the process. It is often called the "House of Quality" (see fig. 5–2). It is called the House of Quality because its shape resembles a house and there are a foundation, walls, and roof, all of which relate to quality concerns. Motorola uses the pizza example in figure 5–2 to show that any service can use it to enhance their quality. This assessment and planning tool provides a graphic means of illustrating customer requirements, design parameters, and the perceived and real differences between a business and its competition. This is the key document that determines what an organization's final product or service characteristic will be.

The other matrix converts information identified in this planning matrix into component characteristics needed to insure the customer's requirements are met. All of these matrices aim to move design and customer requirements down to operational personnel who must produce the products and deliver the services.

While all of these tools are important, the Planning Matrix is the key document. The other three translate this planning and assessment tool in-

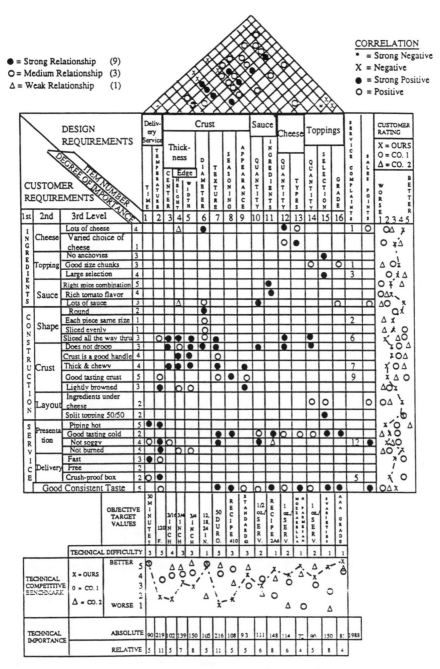

Figure 5–2. Product Planning Matrix

Courtesy of Motorola, Inc.

formation into action. The Planning Matrix provides the focus, the other tools translate the information and then transmit that information throughout the entire design, development, and production process.

As noted earlier, the first step in creating a planning matrix is for the customers to state, in their own terms, what they think are important considerations about the product or service. For instance, a customer may express a desire for dependable service or products. Normally, these requirements would then be described in second- and third-level terms. As seen in figure 5–2, each of these levels seeks further to explain exactly what the customer means. The left-hand vertical side of the matrix is where customer requirements are defined in greater detail. One of the customer requirements in figure 5–2 is construction. This customer requirement is further defined to mean the way a pizza is shaped, its crust, and its layout. Finally, these second-level customer requirements are specifically defined in terms of the way the pizza is cut and so forth.

Any customer requirement can be broken down into more measurable terms. For example, if your customer valued dependability, "dependability" could be further defined to mean "reliable, long-lasting and easily serviced." In the pizza case, dependability might refer to whether each piece is cut to the same size or to the dependability of the delivery service. Customer requirements and definitions are usually derived from market research, customer opinion surveys, and questionnaires, as well as from the input from sales personnel.

The second step in constructing the "House of Quality" or Planning Matrix is to list, across the top horizontal row, what design characteristics should exist in order to meet the customer's requirements. These requirements, as perceived by a business, should relate directly to the customer's requirements. These design characteristics must be directly deployed throughout a business design, assembly, manufacturing, and service process. If they are not, the business has little hope of satisfying customer requirements.

One key requirement is that these design characteristics be measurable so they can be compared to objective targets. Of equal importance is the need to make sure that not only are design characteristics measurable, but that the right characteristics (in terms of what is important to the customer) are being evaluated. If management is measuring something that is not important to the customer, then the business needs to reassess and redefine their objectives.

The third step to creating a "House of Quality" is to identify the relationship between customer requirements and design characteristics. Since there can be varying degrees of correlation between these two variables, the matrix uses three symbols to identify the strength of this relationship. A strong relationship is identified by a solid dot (●), a medium relationship is shown by a hollow dot (○), and the weak relationship's symbol is a triangle (△)

Indexing customer requirements and design characteristics in this manner helps organizations quickly see if other design characteristics are adequately covering customer expectations. If there are no symbol entered or if a majority of the symbols relating to a specific customer requirement are weak, then some of the customer's needs and wants are not being met. In this case, design has little chance of meeting customer expectations. This indexing process makes it possible to identify conflicting design requirements. Relationships—including strongly negative ones—between two design characteristics can be seen in the "roof" of the house of quality.

The fourth step, as seen on the right side of figure 5–2, involves graphing a *market evaluation* or *customer rating* of a business and its competition. Usually this includes some customer ratings, where a business and its competition are compared on each of the variables the customer considers important. This item-by-item comparison helps a business see how they compare, in the customer's eyes, to their competition. Assessing how one "stacks up" against the competition helps managers establish their priorities based on where improvements need to be made. If a competitor fulfills a customer's need better, then this area is a likely target for improvement. On the other hand, such market evaluation can identify possible selling points because the process also shows potential strengths in relation to competitors. Information shown on the market evaluation comes from customer surveys, sales information, and other sources.

Technical Competitive Benchmarking is located on the bottom section of the "House of Quality." Information for this fifth step is normally acquired through in-house tests and evaluations. It is best for these evaluations to be objective and measurable, but if subjective terms are needed, some performance rating should be used. These scores or numbers are then compared to customer or market evaluations shown on the vertical right side of the "House of Quality."

This comparison can help point out any inconsistency that exists between what customers are saying and what a self-evaluation has shown. For example, if a customer evaluation indicates a competitor best meets a specific customer requirement while an in-house evaluation shows the opposite, something is clearly wrong. Either the evaluation process is defective or the customer's needs were not being met because the wrong design characteristics were chosen when the QFD process began.

After these steps have been completed, it then becomes a matter of analyzing the information, determining a business' strengths and weaknesses, and identifying specific selling points. These targeted design characteristics are then communicated throughout the business. Once the "House of Quality" is finished, it is then possible to use a chart called the Deployment Matrix, which describes customer and design characteristics in greater detail so production can identify components needed to satisfy the customer, as well as design requirements.

Once the components are identified, a Process Plan and Control helps push the process from development to production. This involves listing all critical components needed to satisfy requirements and then identifying critical control points. For instance, it may be necessary to use sampling or statistical process control techniques like the mean (x) and range (R) charts to monitor the flow of materials or other control points critical to developing a good component. In turn, this component will be one of several components to provide a final product or service that satisfies both customer and design requirements. Once these critical control points have been identified, it is simply a matter of issuing operating instructions for personnel who must actually perform the work and follow the quality control plan.

Parameter Design

Ford Motor Company, AT&T and Xerox, among others, have used *Taguchi methods* to enhance their products. Taguchi methods were developed through the work of Dr. Genichi Taguchi, who is the executive director of the non-profit organization, American Supplier Institute, Inc., in Dearborn, Michigan. He has received four Deming Prizes and has been a force on the cutting edge of product design. His main contribution has involved combining engineering and statistical methods to achieve rapid improvement in cost and quality by optimizing product design and manufacturing processes.[8]

The aim of the Taguchi methods is to integrate product design and manufacturing process. One of the main ways this is accomplished is by training both design engineers and manufacturing personnel in Taguchi methods. The aim in the tradition of horizontal management is to break down barriers between these two groups.

Dr. Taguchi's systematic approach to quality engineering includes three steps: (1) systems design, (2) parameter design, and (3) tolerance design. Systems design has traditionally been a U.S. strong point, and it was often the Japanese that implemented U.S. design systems. Systems designs refers to the initial production design stage of a product where materials, parts, and initial product parameters are established. Parameter design involves testing various combinations of materials and so forth to find the combination that maximizes production while lowering costs. Tolerance design involves buying better grade materials and "spending" more money, whereas parameter design involves optimizing quality with low-cost materials.[9]

The key step in Dr. Taguchi's quality process is Parameter Design, and a key to understanding his concept of loss and uncontrollable factors. Dr. Taguchi views the loss associated with a product as critical. These losses occur when a product's functional characteristics deviate from desired parameters or values. According to Dr. Taguchi, loss occurs not only when a product falls outside its specifications, but also when it falls *within* its specifications.

The greater the variation, the worse the design. To reduce this loss caused by a poor-quality product, you must produce a product at optimal levels with a minimum of variation in its "functional characteristics." Factors affecting this variation include both controllable and uncontrollable factors. Controllable factors include items like material used and cycle time. Uncontrollable factors are those factors which are extremely difficult, if not impossible, to control. These factors are responsible for most variation from target value. Taguchi emphasizes that the goal of good design is not to focus on common uncontrollable factors because they are very costly, if not impossible to control. Instead of finding and eliminating uncontrollable causes, it is better to remove or reduce the *impact* of the causes.[10]

The classic example of using this parameter design approach occurred in Japan in 1953 when a company was using a new kiln. Tiles being baked inside the kiln had extreme variations in temperature. Tiles on the outside of the stack had a different temperature than those on the inside of the stack. The cause of the problem was uneven temperature within the kiln itself. To eliminate the problem, the company would have to spend a half-million dollars redesigning the kiln. Instead, engineers got together and identified seven major *controllable* factors which they thought could affect the tiles including content of the limestone in the tile, fineness of additives, content of agalmatolite, and so forth. After testing, they discovered that the limestone was the most significant factor affecting the variation in temperatures of the tiles. By increasing the limestone content from 1 to 5 percent and by better managing the other six factors, they reduced the defect problem from 30 percent to less than 1 percent. They also discovered they could eliminate the amount of agalmatolite used in the tiles, which was the most costly ingredient, without affecting the quality of the product.[11]

Dr. Taguchi's parameter design focuses on finding a product's parameter values and operating levels, which are the least sensitive to change in environmental conditions and uncontrollable factors, and treat them separately. At the heart of this process is discovering the interaction between controllable and uncontrollable factors.[12]

Concluding Thoughts

QFD and the Taguchi methods provide a means of effectively translating design into finished products and services. Once a product or service is well designed, it is then necessary to create a production process that runs at maximum effectiveness. A poor design means built-in waste, but a poor production process means not being competitive and not meeting customer expectations. To have an effective production process you must instill high expectations within the production system and then be able to meet those goals.

QFD provides a powerful graphical assessment tool for developing a closer link between the customer requirements and design considerations. This horizontal linkage can provide valuable information for an organization because it can show strengths and weaknesses in the customer–design production network. It can also show how an organization stacks up against its competition and how accurate and relevant design considerations are to customer needs and desires. As such, it provides a way to focus on and solve problems between the functional areas of a business. Enhancing this horizontal communication is necessary in order to deliver products and services that best serve the needs of the customer.

Taguchi methods along with QFD provide a means of both enhancing new designs and improving current designs. Taguchi Parameter Design focuses management's attention on making better use of what exists, rather than coming up with something entirely new. This is often a radical thought to a disposable society like the United States. However, it is often uneconomical to go through a major redesign. It is reassessment of current design and focusing on controllable, as opposed to uncontrollable, variables that frequently result in the most dramatic cost reduction and quality and productivity improvements.

Neither of these methods requires upper management to implement horizontal management, but developing a more horizontal management perspective is a natural outcome of focusing on customers rather than managers or bosses. Powerful customer feedback tools like Taguchi methods and QFD help create a customer perspective by bringing the customer more clearly into managerial decision making.

American Express is doing the same thing with their emphasis on customer transactions. When they started measuring and surveying their managerial performance based on single customer transactions, they began concentrating on the communication links between their functional units. Focusing on these horizontal networks allows vertical organizations the opportunity to reap some of the benefits of horizontal management.

Motorola's Six Sigma approach is somewhat different from American Express's method in that it not only targets customer satisfaction but raises the measure of effectiveness. Any customer is concerned with variation in services and products, but Motorola has gone beyond merely addressing this variation. They are actually trying to anticipate future customer needs and desires. They hope that by raising their expectations, they will be better able to meet those needs.

The real key to meeting customer needs is to concentrate on measuring customer performance as *the* way to improve return on investment. Motorola's "defects per unit" concept provides diverse groups and departments with a common language. Having a common language makes it easier for everyone to put the customer at the center of the company's actions. In the previous chapter Met Life measurement of performance gaps accomplished much the same thing.

So far we have examined how some companies are beginning to adopt a more horizontal perspective. But it is difficult to see how far these organizations are from a truly horizontal management organization. We need a roadmap, some way of classifying organizations based on the degree to which they are implementing Horizontal Management. Only by doing this can we understand and measure what it will take to go beyond simply focusing on the customer to instead achieving the real competitive advantage of horizontal management: a better decision-making and managerial process.

Notes

1. Raymond J. Larkin, "The History of Quality at American Express," *American Productivity Center Quality Forum*, New York, N.Y., 14 July 1987, p. 3.

2. MaryAnne E. Rasmussen, "Service Quality at American Express: Our Most Strategic Weapon," unpublished document, p. 8.

3. Bill Wiggenhorn, "Achieving Six Sigma Quality," *Opportunities* 5, no. 2 (February 1988) p. 2.

4. Mikel J. Harry, "The Nature of Six Sigma Quality," Six Sigma booklet, Motorola.

5. Ibid.

6. Ibid.

7. Bill Smith, "The Motorola Story," In-house publication.

8. *Taguchi Methods*, Special Information Package, American Supplier Institute, Inc., ASI Press.

9. Diane M. Byrne, and Shin Taguchi, "The Taguchi Approach to Parameter Design," in *Taguchi Methods*, p. 2.

10. Ibid., p. 2.

11. *Taguchi Methods*, p. 2.

12. Ibid., p. 2.

Part III
Beyond Customer Satisfaction

6
Boundaries of Horizontal Management

We have already looked at some examples of horizontal management techniques and some ways they have been used by companies like Met Life, Motorola, and American Express. None of these organizations would be classified as a truly horizontal organization, although American Express probably comes closest. Each has some horizontal networks extending through their vertical organization.

At present there is not what I call a level-one, completely flat horizontal organization, but many organizations are developing more horizontal tendencies. Each has boundaries or structural limits to their horizontal development. These limits are defined by three factors: (1) the managerial issues or scope of decision making that lower-level personnel are allowed to participate in; (2) the problem-solving process that is used; and (3) the degree to which members are involved in the process.

Scope

The range of subjects that employees and lower-level managers are involved in can be broad or narrow. The concerns that lower-level personnel can become involved in can be thought of as a continuum ranging from very limited work areas concerns to very broad strategic and investment topics (see figure 6–1). The scope of problem solving and discussions in this continuum ranges from simple concerns for environmental working conditions (e.g. temperature, tool selection, monitoring their own performance) to deciding how work areas will be arranged in relationship to each other. Some lower-level employees even become involved in strategic issues (employee bonus programs, new product lines, or customer relations).

What's the Proper Level?

Figure 6–1 shows the basic steps involved in developing a level-one organization. The figure has a purely vertical organization on the left side of

LEVEL ONE FLAT OR HORIZONTAL ORGANIZATION

Step I	Step II	Step III	Step IV	Step V
	Narrow	to Broad	Decision Making	
Work-Area Subjects	Daily Managerial Matters	Workplace design and Layout Considerations	Financial, Capital and Investment Topics	Strategic Issues
Simple problem investigation and recommendations to problem resolution and implementation				
Participating in employee suggestion programs	Arranging schedules	Cross-training	Deciding capital expenditure	Developing new product lines
Determining work breaks	Delegating work activities	Selecting vendors	Distribution of profit sharing	
Timeclocks, flextime	Determining production rates	Selecting technology		Launching new business ventures
Operational problem solving	Ordering material	Planning equipment utilization	Making investment decisions	
Monitoring quality control charts	Keeping records	Selecting work methods and measurement criteria		Managing inventory systems ("push" or "pull")
Selecting benefits and pension package	Monitoring load reports	Work sampling		
	Establishing statistical control limits	Determining how the workplace will be arranged	Controlling inventory size and turnover	Emphasizing quality vs. productivity issues
	Performing preventative maintenance	Planning capacity		Selecting facility locations
	Allocating punishment, rewards	Master scheduling	Determining Economic Order Quantity and Reorder Points	
	Hiring and firing	Line balancing		
	Allocating manpower	Cutting flow distance and changeover time	Conducting value analysis	
	Forecasting (short term)	Forecasting (intermediate)		Forecasting (long range)

VERTICAL ORGANIZATION

Figure 6–1. Steps of Horizontal Management Continuum

the continuum and a theoretical level-one organization on the right side. In between are a series of steps I through V. These steps represent a range of decision making beginning on the left with very narrow delegation to very broad delegation of decision making on the right. Those decisions on the left primarily consist of narrowly focused work-area subjects.

For purposes of explanation the chart has been divided into these five steps, but obviously some subjects can overlap. For instance, delegation of forecasting responsibilities can occur at several steps. Likewise, preventive maintenance is listed in step II but, depending on the duties, it can and is a part of work-area subjects. The figure is only meant to be used for illustrative purposes and not as the ultimate classification of management subjects.

Organizations that are experimenting with horizontal management techniques usually—but not always—begin with work-area subjects. Those using this step likewise often begin by delegating only problem-investigation and recommendation-making responsibilities. More advanced delegators also allow employees the opportunity to make actual decisions rather than simply asking for their advice.

Therefore, at each step along the way employees can be brought in as full partners in the decision making or only as associates with limited responsibilities. The degree to which managers involve employees in this decision-making process depends on *trust*. As managers begin to trust employees, the degree of employee involvement will change from simple problem investigation to actual decision making. Simple problem investigation and recommendation making can occur at any step on the continuum, but usually it begins by having operational people jointly resolve *work-area subjects*.

The subject matter employees are involved in at this first stage of the continuum include the much maligned employee suggestion programs. Just because its track record has not been the greatest does not mean the technique is flawed. It is how the technique is used that makes the difference. For instance, American Airlines once implemented an employee suggestion program that saved the company $50 million in only twelve weeks of operation. The secret lies in how it was implemented. It was systematic, extensive, and had top management support.[1]

Other subjects in step I where employees have been allowed to participate include determining when to take work breaks. As we shall see, many companies today are doing away with time clocks, a form of distrust, and installing various forms of flextime arrangements. Some are even experimenting with "work at home" flexplace arrangements. Monitoring SPC charts and stopping the production line to make corrections before quality or inventory goes out of control are also popular ways of delegating worker participation. The positive effects of these programs, which increase the distribution of authority and responsibility, have already been noted in Chapter 2.

Once a company's managers have become successful with implementing step I, they often begin experimenting with step II. This involves empowering people to make broader decisions concerning *daily managerial matters*. It is these activities that one normally thinks of as being the domain of first-line managers. Increasingly, both individual employees and teams are making decisions that were once reserved for these managers. There is greater employee involvement in arranging work schedules, delegating responsibilities within the work group, and ordering materials, as well as keeping track of departmental materials and inventory. In some cases, teams of workers also allocate their manpower needs, hire, fire, and reward each other.

As company officials go from using step I to step II, they make a major transition from a vertical to a horizontal arrangement. At step I, additional responsibilities are being added to employees' job duties. No restructuring is occurring; it is still a vertical organization that simply makes better use of its labor force. At step II, there is an actual rearranging, a metamorphosis, starting to occur. Those things that once were the exclusive sphere of management are now being taken over by groups of employee teams.

At step III, horizontal management makes a further transformation. In the typical vertical organization, the duties listed under step III on figure 6–1 are usually performed by middle managers and a cadre of staff specialists. Each specialist, of course, focuses on only his or her particular area of interest. Today, we see companies cross-training many of their specialists to assume greater responsibilities and to develop a wider understanding of the organization's overall needs. Some companies are also creating teams of specialists to decide jointly issues formally decided in a piecemeal approach. One example of this is the effort to bring together marketing specialists, product designers, production people, external customers, and suppliers into product-development decisions.

While most of the activities at step III involve reassigning managerial activities downward there is no reason—given enough information and training—why many of these step III duties cannot be performed by even lower-level employees. This includes greater involvement in vendor and technology selection as well as other planning, scheduling, and control decisions normally reserved for staff and middle managers. It is just a matter of faith in employee capability and intelligence.

Very few people would disagree with the belief that work-area subjects are where employees should have input. In fact, involvement even at this level can be very profitable for an organization. A report by the National Association of Suggestion Systems (NASS) reports that employee suggestion programs saved organizations $2.2 billion in 1988. That was a 10 percent increase just over 1987.[2] Still, there is a great deal of room for improvement here. A survey of Industrial Engineers reports that 75 percent of their respondents said that managers do not seek employee input on decisions about which the employee has knowledge.[3]

In the past, companies have made use of these simple work-area teams to make decisions normally reserved for front-line managers. What we are seeing today is an extension of this horizontal decision making occurring on broader daily managerial issues like hiring, firing, and other managerial activities previously performed by front-line managers. In later chapters we will examine the use of techniques like autonomous work groups and "super teams" that are designed to further flatten the pyramid and to delegate higher-level managerial duties to operational personnel.

Which Way Is Up?

All but the most innovative and cutting-edge organizations are at step III in their horizontal transformation. All but the most farsighted organizations have generally left the medium- and long-range decision making to the realm of middle- and upper-level management. As we shall see, however, that situation is changing rapidly.

Granted, at present it is rare to see cases where even the lowest-level employees are being brought into steps IV and V, but it is occurring. These people are actually beginning to provide input and, in some cases, even decide corporate-wide financial and strategic issues. This includes deciding issues like capital expenditures, which inventory system to use, which product lines to develop, and which venture to pursue. Organizations of the twenty-first century, like SRC and Glaxo, have moved further toward decentralization and worker autonomy than any traditional managers had ever imagined possible. As the hierarchy flattens, a broader group of employees will have a stronger voice in the strategic and financial decisions affecting an organization. The emergence of ESOPs', and PepsiCo's use of stock options for all full-time employees as well as other employee-ownership programs are spreading delegation downward throughout the organization.

Piecemeal approaches never work. It is impossible to implement a horizontal technique such as the use of problem-solving teams and expect it to work unless upper management understands its purpose and function. For any horizontal philosophy to be effective, it is imperative that all parties understand what subjects are to be discussed and analyzed. It must be clear where along the decision-making continuum power to decide will be distributed and who will share the power and to what degree.

Problem Solving

Problem solving usually involves identifying problems, developing possible solutions, selecting a solution, implementing it, and evaluating the results. Even if a subject (say, work rules or quality procedures) is up for discussion, the degree to which "lower-level" personnel can become involved varies dramatically.

Depending on their position, organizational members can become involved in determining what is *causing* a particular problem in the work area. For instance, a problem with quality in terms of rejects or scrap may be identified at a very low operational level, but because of the vertical structure of power, may only be resolved at a much higher level. Certainly the current approach to problem solving of giving the line people first shot at resolving it before assigning it to staff assistance is a horizontal approach.

Giving line personnel first shot at resolving a problem means that they must not only identify the problem, but also become involved in generating solutions to it and planning how to implement decisions and evaluate results. This total problem-solving approach is what worked so well at the operational level for Ford's Employee Involvement (EI) program (which is discussed more fully in a later chapter).

Problem solving occurs on a continuum that ranges from partial to full equity in decision making among the various members of the organization. At a theoretical level, a horizontal organization can have each member fully involved in the entire problem-solving process. Obviously, such a setting is not what we think of as the traditional employee/manager relationship.

Back to the Future

The traditional employee-manager relationship with its built-in inequity is evolving into a more horizontal approach as one can see from the emergence of the terms "associate" and "full member." An organization with total equality among members would have no subordinates, no associates, and no supervisors. The members of such an organization would be equal in rank and power. The greatest resistance to such an idea arises in the belief that there must be direction; there must be a central processing unit. Those who cannot accept the idea of a completely horizontal organization do so because they believe it would have no leadership. There is leadership—it is just that it resides in all the members, not just those in one location.

As we shall see, such an organization is not that farfetched. It is not here yet, but it is certainly possible to describe how such an organization might work. Rather than having any one leader, a level-one organization would have a *floating leadership* where different parts of the organization were engaged for different tasks. It seems obvious that some technological innovations could bring about such an arrangement.

Computers could be used to speed up the communication process. A worker-colleague sends out a query on a computer network that links him to other colleagues around the world. This act would form, in effect, one big brain to solve the problem at hand. Computer Integrated Manufacturing (CIM) and its focus on centralizing and streamlining the paper flow between "islands of automation" may be the forerunner of a computer network designed to control normal daily business. Perhaps something like a computerized Executive Operations System (EOS) could simply process the evaluations from teams of decision makers. These decision-making clusters of people could analyze, evaluate, and recommend choices. The EOS would then simply verify that the decision fits within corporate guidelines. Some companies (see Chapter 9) are already doing this except that they use people rather than computers to make this final verification.

Expert systems and other artificial intelligence systems could enable the organizations to function in a self-regulating fashion like the brain-stem functions of the human body. It would only be when an opportunity or crisis occurs that higher-level (human) decision making would be needed.

Back to the Present

From the twentieth-century standpoint, exactly how close any organization can come to achieving level one or creating an entity composed of equal members depends on several structural limits. The first of which is the knowledge (not intelligence) level of members within the organization. To be full participants in the organization, members must possess both content and process knowledge. If participants only make decisions on relatively insignificant problems instead of on broader design, investment, and strategic issues, it is unlikely that these members will be fully utilized or engaged.

The greater the scope of involvement, the more highly motivated and empowered those participants are likely to be. It is only when workers are involved in the entire decision-making process (e.g. problem identification, developing solutions, and so forth) that they feel truly empowered.

Before anyone can participate they must have the knowledge and skill needed to make intelligent choices. Upgrading the employees' understanding of the financial knowledge is the only way one can make good strategic and investment decisions. We will look at one company that has chosen this powerful strategic weapon that creates total employee involvement (TEI). Traditional layered organizations that run up against companies organized by a TEI strategy will soon be devoured.

Making Choices

Most organizations are not planned, they just happen over time; a little investment here, an acquisition there and a divestiture over there, and *voila*—an organizational fruitcake. Managerial actions often seem just as random. How many times have you heard business leaders or politicians talk about "that vision thing"? Their "vision" usually involves wanting to be "number one" or "the best." That is not vision. At best, that is hope, and, at worst, just idle dreaming. To have a vision, one has to have a plan, some way of operating day to day to achieve the kind of organization desired.

An example of such fuzzy vision can be seen in the comments of Roger Smith, CEO of General Motors. During Smith's tenure, Ford out-earned GM for the first time since the 1920s. GM's share of the U.S. auto market fell from 45 percent in 1981 when Smith took over to 36 percent in 1988. That is a lost market share equivalent to Chrysler's entire output.[4]

When interviewed, Smith said he would make the same decisions he did in 1981 when he became CEO *but* he would do a better job communicating the message and would "make sure they understood my vision."[4] He said the employees would know why he was tearing down the place. He went on to say, "There we were charging up the hill right on schedule and I looked behind me and many people were still at the bottom trying to decide whether to come along."[4]

Perhaps they did not know the way, or perhaps they did not have much reason to go up the hill. Who knows? What is known is that vision is more than simply letting others know what and why you want to do something. It is more than simply wanting to be less autocratic and more participative. You have to visualize clearly what it takes to get there. How does vision translate into action? A coach does not say, "Guys, I want to win. We're the best." Instead, he recruits the right people, trains them, prepares them, focuses on strengths, and decides how to attack the opposition. Wal-Mart, SRC, and Hewlett-Packard have a clear focus, a real vision that can be seen throughout their organizational culture.

Concluding Thoughts

For organizations to reach that hypothetical level one, they must establish complete equality among their workers. This is where all personnel, are involved in the entire decision-making process. Whether it is possible is up for debate. It is a lot closer to reality than people generally realize. Regardless of the debate on this issue, it is abundantly clear that empowerment works and that the spread of managerial responsibility and authority to lower-level employees is occurring at a quickening pace. Departmental walls are falling everywhere. New breeds of organizations staffed by multi-talented, multi-responsible members are emerging. It is an exciting time that companies can turn into their competitive advantage.

Although little data is available, most experimenting with horizontal management appears to be between steps I and II. In this book, we examine many companies that have moved well beyond this starting point.

They are on the cutting edge of empowerment and competitiveness. It is up to each of us to decide what it is that we want. Unlike the casino vice-president in Chapter 1, one must first decide what is possible and what is desirable before attempting to empower people; otherwise, it will be one more useless piecemeal management approach.

Before implementing Total Quality Management, Just-In-Time, Quality Circles, Quality of Life, NOAC, or a maze of other horizontal techniques, managers should decide what they want to do and what they believe. Do you believe that getting operational people involved in decision making increases employee satisfaction and reduces resistance to change? If you do, you are a human-relations person and will, at best, probably reserve employee participation to step I in the horizontal continuum.

If you believe that delegating autonomy, responsibility and authority results in *better decisions,* then you are a human-resources person. Many managers with this attitude, as we shall see, are already implementing steps II and III. Some are even at various stages of implementing steps IV and V. On the other hand, if you believe that full participation in the workplace is the God-given right of all people, then you are an egalitarian or democratic person. In this case, it is possible to reach level one, but it will be an evolutionary process dependent on employee development and advances in technology.

The higher the level of decisions, like strategic or investment decisions (steps IV and V), that are delegated to participants, the closer the organization comes to becoming a level one horizontal organization. The more systematic the use of horizontal management techniques, the closer a company approaches horizontal structure.

Notes

1. D. Keith Denton, *Quality Service* (Houston, Tex.: Gulf Publishing Company, 1989), p. 109.

2. "I.E. Newsfront," *Industrial Engineering,* August 1989, p. 6.

3. "Productivity and Quality Survey," *Focus: Industrial Engineering,* April 1990, p. 8.

4. Woods Wilton, "The U.S. Must Do As G.M. Has Done," *Fortune,* 13 February 1989, p. 71.

7

Culture and Scope of Horizontal Management

Determining whether an organization has a horizontal structure is not a yes or no proposition. Almost all organizations have some horizontal aspects; the question is to what degree. It can range from the delegating of simple preventative maintenance procedures to the shop floor to employee involvement in strategic decision making. The extent to which an organization is able to develop a horizontal culture depends on several variables, some obvious and some not so obvious.

Variables Affecting Change

Commitment

The first variable affecting the degree of horizontal structure within an organization is an obvious one, namely *top management commitment.* Things just do not go very far without the CEO's support. In some cases it is not enough to insure change, but in all cases, it is essential for long-term change. It is unlikely that middle or front-line management would support horizontal initiatives like NOAC unless they see that top management is serious about the concept.

There must be strong evidence that upper management is providing more than simple lip service to the concept. Often the attitude of middle-level managers is like that echoed by one cynical middle manager who said, "Top management is like a bunch of sea gulls. They come in, 'squawk' a lot, mess all over your place, then leave!" Those words came from a manager who worked for a corporation that had a good reputation for employee relations!

Most middle- and lower-level managers have heard it all before, so if upper managers are serious about a change to a more horizontal mode of operation, they will have to prove it. In a moment we will look at how Ford Motor Company was able to convince highly resistant managers and an extremely cynical group of employees to adopt a more horizontal arrangement with Employee Involvement (EI) as the centerpiece of a new competitive strategy.

Patience

Along the same lines is the fact that any change, especially one like horizontal management that involves a structural and cultural "perestroika," is going to take time. *Investing the time* is essential because it takes time to re-organize people and resources. It takes time to get an operation up and running.

All too often the CEO or other top official simply wants to "hit the ground running." That may be fine for something like introducing a new product line, but cultural changes are not something that you can bring about by hiring a pop-psych consultant, giving employees one hour of hype and two hours of training, and then implement and expect to see a return-on-investment (ROI) in three months. It seems ridiculous, but I have known cases where exactly that was the expectation. Implementing a horizontal process will have little chance of success if the necessary time is not allocated for training and coordination.

Ford's successful EI efforts have been going on for over ten years, and they are still making changes and improvements. Perhaps one of the biggest surprises coming from this highly automated, highly engineered corporation that normally evaluates programs based on scientific measurement and methods was what they did not do. From the very beginning Ford decided *not* to measure the results of the EI process. Ford's management involved in EI knew it would take time. They decided not to expect immediate results—not even to measure them. That may have been the single most important thing they did to insure its success.

Legitimacy

Any change must be perceived as legitimate if it is to be successful. Legitimizing the change both increases the satisfaction with the concept and improves the performance of individuals affected by the concept. Those involved in developing a more horizontal culture need to perceive NOAC, participative management, EI, Autonomous Work Groups, or other horizontal approaches as legitimate and congruent with the current leadership style. Policies, training, and compensation schedules must be redesigned to create the proper atmosphere of expectation in every worker.

At Ford this initial legitimization was critical, so a joint implementation committee was established. The first National Joint Committee on Employee Involvement was chaired jointly by vice-president of Labor Relations at Ford and the United Auto Workers (UAW) vice-president and director of the Ford Department. A policy letter on EI was issued by the president of Ford, Phillip Caldwell, and the resources of Ford's Employee Relations staff were redirected to support EI efforts.

During that same time Don Peterson, then president of Ford, invited Dr. Edward Deming to advise them on quality. It was during these meetings that Deming emphasized that management, not labor, was the root of their problems. Paul A. Banas, manager of Employee Development and Planning at Ford, gives credit to Deming for helping Ford redefine their company's definition of quality based on the customer's requirements. Banas emphasized that this was a significant shift in thinking at Ford. Up to this point, Ford managers had always believed 80 percent of the company's problems were caused by employees.[1]

Ford legitimized EI by inviting people like Deming to speak, as well as taking numerous trips to study the methods of Japanese automakers. They realized that the competitive advantage does not depend on technology. The solution to their problem depended on the company's ability to tap their work force's competencies, capacities, and commitment.[2]

Introducing a horizontal management philosophy is most effective if it is integrated into the day-to-day aspects of the organization. One of the most obvious ways of legitimizing these new concepts is to tie extrinsic and intrinsic rewards directly into some horizontal approach. In Ford's case, they provided employees with some of the most powerful incentives available. Ford and their union, the UAW, *jointly* decided where to focus EI training efforts and how training would be set up. This was a step V or strategic issue that both the union and management were involved in. Even daily decision making was considered a joint proposition.

Training

People need information about the problems they are expected to identify and solve. They need the proper training to be able to participate in a meaningful fashion. In other words, *they must know how to contribute.* The skills and information participants have about the process of implementing horizontal management techniques are essential to success. If a manager or employee lacks the necessary skills or information about an activity or program, they will often fail to become involved. If they do become involved, their involvement will often be of a token nature and of little significance.

On the other hand, if participants do have the necessary skills and information, it produces higher personal satisfaction and performance. The lesson here is that before implementing any horizontal approach, identify *relevant* information about the problems participants are expected to identify and solve. Do they know what is involved? For instance, employees could not be expected to solve budgetary, investment, or strategic issues if they had never been exposed to these. This type of knowledge is sometimes referred to as "content knowledge."

Participants also need to have so-called process knowledge about how to operate a horizontal management technique or philosophy (NOAC, SPC, JIT, EI). Often this essential area is overlooked. Participants need problem-solving knowledge and skills so they can identify problems, generate possible solutions, make decisions, and communicate results.

In Ford's EI efforts, there were problem-solving teams that looked at a broad array of problems from those affecting quality of work life to those affecting the quality of the product. Quality circles focused almost exclusively on product quality. Ford's problem-solving teams received training in such things as team building, generic problem solving, and presentation skills. Quality-circle groups were trained in cause-effect diagrams, graphs, Pareto diagrams, basic statistics, and presentation skills.[3]

Sharing

The greater the gap in status between organizational levels, the lower the amount of participation. This is especially true of lower-status individuals. Power and position inequities that are too great intimidate lower-level employees and limit their participation. Implementing horizontal management requires that power and status be shared. Employee involvement and commitment are very weak in an organization with stratified status levels. The more people differentiate themselves by status, the less likely it is that management will be able to engage lower-status participants.

This does not necessarily imply that reducing the number of hierarchial levels is the only way to foster equality. Status can and does come from information and knowledge. Reducing the gap in knowledge between management levels increases employee involvement. If it is impossible to reduce the number of levels in the hierarchy, then it is extremely important to make sure that different hierarchial levels, or the ones with very different levels of relevant information, are not members of the same group. Otherwise, full involvement and participation are highly unlikely.

Ford got upper management and the top union leadership to accept their form of employee participation by encouraging skeptics to visit their facilities which had implemented some form of EI. They noted the greatest impact on attitudes occurred when upper management and union officials had the opportunity to talk to their respective peers about the program.[4]

Ford is still a vertical organization, but their EI efforts have been successful mainly because they were successful at creating a long-term major change in their basic managerial style and in their relationships with their union. It is less adversarial now with more joint management activities between the union and Ford. This was evidenced by a study Ford conducted in 1986. Their Employee Communication Survey scientifically analyzed a cross section of 3200 hourly and salaried employees. Three out of four employees recognized Ford was trying harder than earlier to keep employees informed. They found that 58 percent of the employees had participated in EI efforts and 67 percent of those surveyed knew a fair amount to a great amount about EI. More than 80 percent believed employee participation is good for them and their company. Despite the challenge of changing the traditional manager-employee relation, Ford shows it can be done.

Confidence

People will become involved in change if they feel their managers trust them. Managers who do not have confidence in their subordinates or the participative program are less likely to share decision making or to use horizontal management approaches. That was an initial problem for Ford. Ford Managers conducted a Salaried Employee Opinion Survey in the early 1980s and found that only 20 percent of their employees felt confidence and trust was placed in them. The feeling was probably grounded in fact if their managers were typical of other authoritarian American managers. Some years ago a survey of 40,000 managers reported that fewer than 20 percent of those surveyed had a consistent belief in the basic competency of their employees.

If managers show confidence in their subordinates, both the satisfaction and desire to participate increase. This was reflected in Ford's survey of 748 hourly EI participants that indicated 82 percent of those participants were satisfied with their jobs. This compares to 58 percent for those who were satisfied before they became involved in EI. The survey also noted 82 percent of EI participants believe the change accomplished something worthwhile, in contrast to 27 percent who felt this way before EI.[5] When Ford decided to share their decision making, they displayed the ultimate trust and confidence.

Process

Incentives can actually be counterproductive unless they are well thought out. If participants see their participation as insignificant, or if they perceive the activities to be of little value, then the whole effort will be counterproductive. Incentives to change must be planned out in well-conceived stages. Change is not something upper management can simply direct. Paul Banas notes, many employee-involvement, quality-of-life, and quality-circle efforts seem to be conceived as something that top management tells lower management to do. These kinds of efforts are never sustained.[6] Change should be thought of as a *process* not a program, otherwise it is certain to fail.

The necessity of adopting such a stance was pointed out by Banas. He described the poignant remarks of one of the members of their problem-solving groups who said, "I have been involved in many programs over the past twenty years to make improvements in the workplace, and none of them have ever lasted. Again, you raised my expectations with employee involvement. It has made me feel good about coming to work. If this turns out to be just another program, I will never trust you again."

Any change will be successful only if the people involved believe their participation will bring about change. If they do not believe their partici-pation has an effect, it can actually create a negative attitude. It is as if they think, "I used to think I didn't count. Now I know I don't." Many suspect that they do not count. They think the little guy is just that—insignificant.

They obviously do matter. The front-line people primarily make it possible to get those incremental improvements so essential to sustained productivity. It is management's responsibility to show others that they do matter. Middle managers, supervisors, and employees must not only be trained in horizontal management methods, they must believe in both the process and the ability of their subordinates; otherwise, it is a waste of time. This is similar to the problem Ford faced when they introduced their EI process. It took a lot of persistence before their efforts paid off.

Involving Front-Line Managers and Professionals

Progress was slow in the early years of Ford's EI process, but hourly em-ployees gradually became involved in EI projects. Some quality circles were formed at local facilities, but there was considerable resistance, especially from managerial personnel. Ford's initial attempts to get people involved proved disappointing. They decided they needed to determine the problem and what could be done about it. In 1982 they began to examine these reasons and conducted pilot studies to isolate those problems.

What they discovered (and a lesson for all those wanting to implement horizontal management) was that simply formulating a mission was not enough. They found that their managers generally were not committed to the change. These managers told them that participation takes too much time in relation to the benefits, and that their own bosses were more likely to act as barriers than to reward them for practicing this new participative leadership style.[7]

To combat this resistance to change, Ford organized a series of con-ferences. These conferences were designed to help Ford's upper management better understand the problems facing managers trying to implement a more participative management style and to encourage front-line management to become committed to EI. Between 1984 and 1987, Ford sponsored 115 conferences with nearly 4,000 managers in attendance.

They began these conferences by conducting force-field analysis to help managers analyze and clarify, in each manager's eyes, what forces were encouraging and discouraging participative management. These managers found that external factors, including foreign competition, greater customer expectations, and so forth, were encouraging participation. Generally, it was internal conditions, those under the manager's control, which were preventing participative management.

The conferences were designed to confront these restraining forces. One way they did this was to ask managers anonymously to list on cards, "the way we do things around here." They would then review the responses on a flip chart. Items impeding cultural change included responses such as "the boss is always right," "make the facts fit the boss's theories," "play it safe," "don't rock the boat," and so on. Through frank discussions like these, managers began to realize what their culture was and their impact upon it.

As their managers began to realize the role they played in their current culture, they were given the Myers-Briggs Temperament Indicator (MBTI). This seventy-item self-analysis profiles leadership temperament. It identifies four categories: the Promoter, the Traditionalist, the Visionary, and the Democrat.

While the percentages of Visionary and Democratic managers at Ford were approximately those of the normative population, this was not the case for the other two leadership styles. Only 1 percent of Ford's managers were identified as Promoters, while 76 percent were identified as Traditionalists. That these categories were at opposite ends of the scale is an indication of the culture at Ford. The Promoter, which was underrepresented, is the leader that prefers change, one who would most likely accept a shift to horizontal management. The Traditionalist, which was overrepresented, prefers the status quo. Clearly, Ford had a culture that resisted change.

After the survey, Ford management discussed the results with their participating managers. Conference leaders emphasized how the Traditionalist tends to prefer stability and caution and that all leadership temperaments have their own strengths and weaknesses. They noted that all styles can be complementary and mutually beneficial as long as the impact of each style is understood. They went on to explain that each person's natural preference can be overcome when the need calls for it.[8]

These conferences dramatized the need for EI through an exercise called "The Aggressive Corporation." This simulation underscores the point that maximum corporate profits are obtained when there is total cooperation among departments and when profits are divided equally among departments. Total conflict provides the exact opposite. The simulation helped demonstrate the effect such attitudes have on the corporation. Ford trainers observed that, as the years go by, the profits of the Aggressive Corporation tend to go up, and they hope this simulation reflects the real-life state of affairs within the company.[9]

Their trainers also recognized that many of the participating managers were concerned about participative management taking too long. These managers also felt that making all decisions by consensus could do more harm than good. Conference organizers emphasized that consensus in all situations could cause harm, but that consensus was not required in all situations. Instead, there are a wide range of options available to the manager.

These options included *consultative* approaches where managers simply request information and opinions. Using this approach, managers are able to gain the advantage of understanding employee thinking. Since employees have little commitment in this situation, managers must make sure each employee understands the scope of the problem.

Conference leaders also stressed that in some cases managers could use a *collaborative* approach where employees' ideas and concerns were discussed with the manager. The idea is to make both manager and employee feel like winners.

Participants were also shown the advantages of the *delegative* approach where managers outline for employees what is expected and what constraints exist. Responsibility and accountability are assigned, and then the manager pursues other critical matters. Most importantly, conference leaders tried to emphasize that the best participative approach is contingent on the situation.

This contingency approach was demonstrated by using the Vroom-Yetton model of leadership. Using this model, conference organizers helped their managers decide when and to what extent they should involve subordinates in decisions. During this analysis, participants examined consultative, collaborative, and delegative decision-making approaches and learned how to choose among them.

Some of the factors affecting their choice of leadership styles included the need for acceptance of decisions and the amount of time needed to make a decision. In addition to short-circuiting concerns about consensus, conference leaders explored *positive feedback tools* for increasing employee effectiveness and examined how managers can get subordinates involved in planning, goal-setting, and problem-solving activities. Conference organizers told their managers that surveys of Ford employees since 1973 have shown that employees were dissatisfied with the amount of recognition they were receiving. Then the discussions focused on the power of positive feedback.

The Crisis at Ford

Ford's experience with EI provides a striking example of the power of developing a horizontal network, even within a highly vertical organization. It also shows that EI can be a powerful tool to implement horizontal management.

In 1978, Ford Motor Company actually recalled more cars than they built.[10] Less than ten years later, they had the best quality of any U.S. automaker. To understand how EI created this change, you have to go back to 1979.

In the 1970s Ford, in the style typical of U.S. automakers, was noted for their adversarial and rigid relations between management and labor. It was a reputation earned through decades of distrust and dislike. Moreover, as long as profits were good and the economy was strong, there was little reason to change.

Business conditions declined in the late 1970s and early 1980s. The economy was depressed. There was a real crisis. Foreign competition was strong. Market share was being eroded. Hundreds of thousands of employees were being laid off, and Ford's North American operation alone was losing $1.2 billion. It was a time that was ripe for change. Something had to be done.

Ford and their union, the UAW, knew the crux of their quality and profit problem was the way it was managed. It was no longer possible to survive with an "us against them" attitude. This highly structured vertical organization had to change directions. Management and labor had to focus their energies not on each other, but on better satisfying their external customer. They also recognized that in order to enhance quality and customer satisfaction, they had to get the whole organization working together. Employees, as well as management, had to be committed to the change. It meant a drastic change in thinking.

In 1979, Ford and the UAW began discussions to increase the participation and involvement of employees in work matters. In October of 1979, Ford and the UAW signed a letter of agreement in which both organizations agreed jointly to administer employee involvement in an effort to make work more satisfying, to improve the overall work environment, to encourage creativity, to improve quality and efficiency, and to reduce absenteeism.

Implementing this philosophy posed a significant challenge. Changing an essentially adversarial and traditionally authoritarian culture, typical of a highly vertical organization, to one that is more participative and built on mutual trust, respect, and openness is one of the greatest challenges that an organization can face. It is doubtful that anyone at Ford would honestly say the process has been fully implemented. Perhaps Ford never will achieve a completely horizontal structure, but significant progress has already been made.

Progress is seen in the fact that instead of being in serious financial trouble, they are setting record profits and their quality has improved. Paul A. Banas believes their participative management and employee involvement program has directly contributed to their 65 percent improvement in quality between 1980 and 1986, and their record-breaking profits in 1987 and 1988.

Ford's Eight-Step Process

Ford's initial EI emphasis was on encouraging employee involvement groups (problem-solving groups, new-product launch teams, etc.). Then the company provided its employees with the necessary training and education. Ford soon realized that if EI was to be successful, the corporation had to have a more participative culture. They believed their managers had to provide more participative opportunities, not only for their hourly employees, but also for their technical and professional people. Ford's management believed this participation did not and should not always be consensus decision making, but some type of participation must occur.

In order to achieve this participative culture, Ford believed its managers had to have the skills, knowledge, and desire to provide those opportunities to participate. Once this was accomplished, it would still be necessary for systems and processes to be installed that actively encouraged employee involvement in planning, goal setting, problem solving and decision making.

Ford's solution was the *Eight Basic Steps for Launching EI*. A diagram of this process is seen in figure 7–1. The purpose of this system was to insure EI's success.

As figure 7–1 clearly shows, Ford believes that the first step to successfully launching EI is gaining the support and commitment of management, front-line supervisors, and employees because they are the ones who must implement it. Ford emphasized this point in 1982 when they issued the "Letter of Understanding on Training for Employee Involvement." This policy statement pointed out the need to sustain education and training of plant managers and union representatives in participative concepts and skills. It provided the foundation for their management conferences that have already been discussed.

From Ford's viewpoint, the second step for launching EI (and a critical step toward horizontal management) is to make sure that both employees and management are seen as *equal partners* in the venture. At Ford they did this by jointly planning and implementing EI through their Joint Steering Committee. The Steering Committee provided an excellent way for

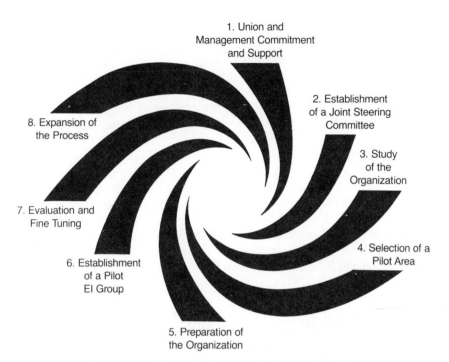

Figure 7–1. Eight Basic Steps for Launching EI

Used with permission of the Ford Motor Company, Inc.

management and labor to cooperate with each other. This committee spent a great deal of its time training the people who have to actually run the daily EI activities. The success of the problem-solving teams in this process hinges on the talents and abilities of these people.

Ford stresses that the relationship between these EI coordinators and facilitators and the Joint Steering Committee is most effective when there is a full partnership between them. This relationship should be a collaborative one involving joint interaction, discussion, planning, and decision making. It is also important for this Steering Committee to stay in touch and to respond promptly to the efforts of EI problem-solving teams. Anything less would demonstrate a lack of management commitment to the process.

The third and fourth steps involve diagnosis and planning. The Joint Steering Committee gathers information and identifies needs and opportunities. The objective is to identify future goals and then make plans to achieve them.

Related to the planning stage is the fifth step, Preparation of the Organization. This step helps insure that expectations for EI are realistic. For example, obviously training and orientation will be necessary for success-ful implementation. Ford concludes this should consist of developing skills in problem solving, information sharing, and listening, as well as other techniques for helping guarantee EI team effectiveness. The company also believes a needs assessment that specifically identifies training needs at each location can enhance the EI process. Some of the training that has proven vital includes an orientation process for *all* union and company leaders and training EI team leaders in listening and group process skills.

The sixth step in their process is the actual implementation stage. Most of Ford's locations used problem-solving teams in their initial exper-iment with EI. The main value they see for establishing a pilot EI group, like the problem-solving teams, is that it helps build relationships within the organization. Initial EI pilot groups or teams also tend to improve the work environment, create better job satisfaction and respect, and open up communication within the organization.

The members of EI pilot teams need time and training in order to adjust to one another. Management should be responsive to EI team pro-posals, even if the team's suggestions or recommendations cannot be ac-cepted. When suggestions cannot be implemented, care must be taken to *explain* why this is the case. Slow responses or inadequate reasons dem-onstrate a lack of commitment to EI.

Initial EI teams can run out of problems to solve. If this is the case, the Joint Steering Committee may assess the situation and decide whether to rotate members or simply change directions. The committee may even recommend new subjects for the problem-solving teams to tackle. In other cases, the problems may become very complex. In this case, the committee may ask management for special resource people to help (personnel, en-gineering). In fact, Ford has generally found that support groups like en-gineering, quality control, and finance can greatly enhance a team's ability to implement recommendations.

The final two steps in launching EI are Evaluating and Fine Tuning and Expansion of the Process, which is a way build acceptance of EI as a way of doing business. To be successful, EI participants must have the freedom to experiment without worrying about mistakes. However, it also means having the teams, coordinators, and facilitators address the tough questions. Questions like "Is it working?" "Is EI achieving its goals?" and "What should be done differently?" are essential and must be asked if EI is to improve continuously.

In the end, EI's success requires that the process become accepted as a way of doing things. It must become woven into the very fabric of every-day business. For this to occur, everyone in the organization must see the need to change and improve. They must be willing and committed to put in the time and effort to accomplish the change.

Follow-through on EI Efforts

Once EI is started, management can begin to look at how to enhance the effectiveness of the EI process. *Ford's Employee Involvement Handbook II* notes that the continuing success of EI depends first on identifying a vision for the way you would like things to be done.[11] This idea should become the benchmark for future efforts. Once the idea has been conceptualized, the next step is to create a Joint Steering Committee. Its primary function is to oversee EI projects and to start up pilot problem-solving teams. These teams will tackle specific production, maintenance, and quality-control problems. Some of the different types of EI teams in operation at Ford are seen in table 7–1.

The EI process includes the use of EI Coordinators/Facilitators. These people work either full- or part-time to help facilitate weekly meetings of the various teams within the EI process. They can be either hourly or salaried volunteers trained in group-facilitation skills. Usually they are responsible for interfacing with various support groups. Currently at Ford, there are 175 union and management appointed facilitators working full time to make EI function.

Other EI committees may be formed as needed. Their purpose would be to maintain the process, act on EI proposals, and plan for the expansion of EI. The Joint Steering Committee itself may form subcommittees as needed for communication, training, monitoring, or other special tasks.

Special effort is needed to make sure that the first-line supervisor's role is enhanced. After all, they are the ones who must help create a positive climate of trust, honesty, commitment, respect, and recognition and reward. Ford recommends that supervisors and EI team members go through the training together. Table 7–2 shows a checklist to improve the operation of the Joint Steering Committee, EI coordinators, EI teams, supervisors, and others involved in EI.

Concluding Thoughts

No one would suggest that Ford has become a level-one horizontal organization, but effective application of EI techniques is a key component to any organization wishing to develop a more horizontal organization. As such, Ford's EI process is a good model for implementing change on the scale needed to implement horizontal management.

Paul A. Banas believes that employee commitment and cooperation at all levels is the "bedrock of all corporate strategies," and that plans for the future will succeed or fail, depending on how well all employees respond.

Table 7–1
Employee Involvement Teams at Ford

Problem-Solving Teams. These are the cornerstone of EI efforts. They deal directly with a specific issue or process that affects production, maintenance, quality, safety and so forth.

Opportunity Teams. These are ad hoc in nature. Usually they are created because of upcoming work related changes (e.g. new technology, product change, facility modifications).

Special-Project Teams. Usually these teams are organized around a special event (e.g. open house, auto show).

Linking Teams. Often these teams consist of representatives from several problem-solving teams. Usually these people deal with systems issues that cross department or shift lines. They are also sometimes used for information-sharing purposes.

Sunset Teams. Usually these groups are formed because of something that occurred in the problem-solving teams. These members may not be formal members of the EI process but they have an interest in a specific topic under discussion. Often a problem-solving team member is a member of this group. Their purpose is to keep them informed of action of the team that affects their immediate work area.

Launch Teams. These are created in the final stages of product or process development. They are designed to improve communication and bridge groups who are vital to the success of the effort (e.g. production design).

Employee Assistance Groups. These are designed to assist and support employees who have attendance and drug and alcohol abuse problems.

Vendor Quality Teams. Vendor Quality Teams meet with vendors or outside company representatives downstream to discuss relative decisions, issues, and solutions.

Source: UAW-Ford Employee Involvement Handbook II: Concepts and Ideas for Continuing Progress. Used with permission of the Ford Motor Company.

Table 7–2
Checklist to Improve Operations

Joint Steering Committee Functioning

We take visible actions to continually demonstrate our joint commitment to EI.

Our Committee meets regularly.

We have direct, personal experience with EI Team members.

We have clearly established our role in the change process.

We have established a common understanding of our relationship with our EI Coordinator/Facilitator.

We have a good idea of where we're headed, when we want to get there, and what we want to accomplish.

Membership is reasonably balanced and includes key union and management leadership.

If other union or management leaders need greater involvement in EI planning, implementation, and monitoring, we have opened a way for their participation.

We maintain a separation between collective bargaining matters and EI.

We distinguish the issues that fall outside the role of EI and deal with them in the proper forum (e.g., Mutual Growth Forum or collective bargaining process).

We communicate with openness and trust.

Our committee has received adequate training to understand, plan, and implement change.

We assure that adequate resources are provided to expand at a planned pace.

We keep in touch with other locations and share ideas on how to improve our EI process.

We have a good common understanding of the status of the EI process in our facility.

We know which employees wish to be involved and have provided opportunities for their participation.

Table 7–2 continued

We have learned how to work together as a team on EI matters.

Our process of working as a committee is efficient and effective.

Our decisions are implemented in a timely way.

When we experience setbacks or plateaus, we reassess the situation and take appropriate corrective actions.

In addition to problem-solving teams, we are using other forms of involvement.

EI Coordinators/Facilitators

Have received appropriate initial and ongoing training as quickly as possible.

Are encouraged and allowed to attend EI-related conferences, seminars, and workshops.

Share their learnings with the committee and other appropriate persons.

Communicate EI activities broadly throughout the plant (e.g., newsletters, bulletin boards, committee and EI Team minutes).

Function collaboratively with the committee to keep the process on track.

Are not expected to carry out their responsibilities for the EI process without active help from committee members and plant support groups.

Are accorded due respect and recognized for their efforts and accomplishments.

Feel their role in the process is sufficiently clear and not in conflict with expectations of other groups.

Provide adequate training and facilitation to EI Teams.

Ensure that the committee is informed of the "health" of EI Teams and other EI projects.

Develop training materials to meet local needs.

Table 7–2 continued

EI Teams

Are accomplishing worthwhile things.

Meet regularly with good attendance.

Have good spirit.

Have been adequately trained for their stage of development.

Receive sufficient information and assistance from support groups.

Receive adequate and timely responses to proposals.

Are allowed adequate time and space to meet.

Are provided recognition for their efforts.

Supervisors, Managers and Support Groups

Understand and accept their responsibilities to support EI activities, even though they themselves might not be directly involved.

Have received training in EI and are examining their roles in supporting EI.

Form and join EI Teams in their own areas and participate in other EI activities whenever they can.

Have a forum to resolve problems related to EI.

Provide adequate and timely responses to EI Team proposals.

Have adequate freedom to carry out their EI responsibilities.

Provide adequate and timely information in support of EI.

Try to resolve employee problems quickly and rationally.

Committee Persons

Are provided adequate and timely information regarding pending decisions and actions related to the EI process that could affect them and their constituents.

Are provided opportunities to participate and contribute to the Steering Committee, subcommittees, and area EI committees.

Table 7–2 continued

Are afforded EI-related training and education.

Attend representative EI Team meetings to get firsthand knowledge of team activities and provide assistance and guidance.

All Other Employees

Are provided opportunities to participate if they want to.

Are allowed sufficient avenues to resolve work-related problems.

Are kept informed about EI and EI activities.

Are kept informed about relevant plant information (e.g., schedules, performance indicators).

Are asked for information regarding decisions that will affect their jobs.

Are asked for information on subjects about which they are knowledgeable.

Source: *UAW-Ford Employee Involvement Handbook II: Concepts and Ideas for Continuing Progress.* Used by permission of Ford Motor Company.

He also notes that the real key to the future will depend on managers learning how to obtain this employee commitment.

Ford, a highly vertical organization, has gained greater employee commitment through their EI process. They have taken a systems approach and used a variety of EI techniques to enhance both employee commitment and their own global competitiveness. Still, their techniques would have been even more powerful within a horizontal organization designed to increase the importance of operational-level people.

Many organizations preach the benefits of employee involvement; just as many state the importance of customer satisfaction. However, most achieve neither because they fail to implement an effective corporate strategy to achieve either of these goals. Ford provides a shining example of what can be done when both the desire and resources are available. They are taking a traditional autocratic organization and gradually turning it into one that has a competitive culture that makes better use of its most valuable resource—its people. It is not perfect, and it may never be complete, but that is what continuous improvement is all about. They have benchmarked their competition, assessed what changes they need to make, and are actively changing the way they do business. Ford's EI approach, combined with more horizontal perspective, could help any organization greatly enhance the competitive posture within the global marketplace.

Notes

1. Paul A. Banas, "Ford's Transformation: The Role of Employee Involvement and Participative Management," *26th IRC Symposium on Advanced Research in Industrial Relations,* 18 August 1988, pp. 6.

2. Ibid., p. 14.

3. Paul A. Banas, "Employee Involvement: A Sustained Labor/Management Initiative at the Ford Motor Company," in *Productivity in Organization: New Perspectives from Industrial and Organizational Psychology,* ed. John P. Campbell, Richard J. Campbell (San Francisco: Jossey-Bass Publishing, 1988), pp. 396–409.

4. Ibid.

5. Banas, p. 9.

6. Ibid.

7. Paul A. Banas, and Raymond Savers, *Participative Management and Employee Involvement Model and Application,* Ford Motor Company, February 1988.

8. Ibid.

9. Ibid.

10. Banas, p. 5.

11. *UAW-Ford Employee Involvement Handbook II: Concepts and Ideas for Continuing Progress,* The UAW-Ford National Ford Department and Labor Relations Staff, Ford Motor Company., 1983.

8
Streamlining: Eliminate, Simplify, and Combine

For anyone who is seriously considering the notion of horizontal structure, there is one question that comes to mind—decision making. One might say, "In theory the idea of delegation and expanded participative opportunities is not that difficult to support nor justify." After all, various forms of participative management and employee involvement have, to a greater or lesser degree, been around for a very long time. Mass efforts at purposely trying to establish a horizontal structure within the organization is a recent phenomenon. As the levels of the organization decrease it makes significant changes in the relationship between organizational members and rearranges the power structure.

If you carry the concept of a horizontal management structure to its logical end, you inevitably end up with the potential for a level-one horizontal management structure. As you near this theoretical level one, the concern for the decision-making process becomes more urgent. As long as horizontal management simply consists of overlaying and intertwining a horizontal decision-making network throughout the organization, then there is little urgency about how decisions will be made. They are simply made the old-fashioned boss-to-employee way. Horizontal management networks within a traditional management structure are simply an auxiliary or supplemental decision-making process.

It is only when horizontal management begins to convert from this auxiliary decision making to main-drive decision making that one faces the ultimate question, "Exactly *how will the day-to-day decisions be made in a completely horizontal organization?*" The first response might be, "Who cares, we do not have to figure that out yet. We'll get to it if we ever reach theoretical level one." The question cannot be dismissed so easily. Long before a large organization reaches level one the decision-making process has to begin to change. As organizations become flatter, the change in the decision-making process is already taking place.

The Elimination of Decision Making

Explanations, examples, and illustrations of how this type of decision-making process can occur, and is in fact occurring on smaller scales, will be reviewed in succeeding chapters. For now, we should first make one point. In flat horizontal structures it may be that day-to-day decisions are not made at all, at least not in the traditional sense.

This is summarized in the title of this chapter, "Eliminate, Simplify, and Combine." This phrase is often referred to as the engineering approach to problem solving. Rather than assume decisions have to be made, assume they do not. The majority of decision making occurring in organizations is not necessary; it is redundant, and often has already taken place in the past or at the operational level. If there were greater efficiency or trust, many decisions would not have to be made. Many decisions are procedural, routine, and automatic.

A great deal of efficiency, not to mention delegation and operational autonomy, could be gained simply by not decision re-making. How many times has a front-line supervisor or worker discovered a problem and known what to do, but had to wait for management's approval? Think of all the routine decisions that could be made daily.

If a customer wants a loan, approval should be a matter of making sure that customer meets the criteria. If he or she does, the loan is approved; if not, it isn't. Most decision making in corporations is or should be highly mechanical. It should be just a matter of following the standard procedures, rules, and regulations. A machine could do it, perhaps even better than some of the "warm bodies" some businesses pull off the streets to do the job.

Before worrying about who is going to make a decision, we should first decide if we need to make the decision at all. There are no figures on this question, but I would bet that at least 90 percent of all decisions made in an organizations are really unnecessary. This validation of the decision-making process is essentially what General Electric (G.E.) is currently going through in a process called "Work Out," which is intended to streamline their operation and empower their employees.

Any time there is more than one course of action to be taken, a decision has to be made. There will always be alternatives—the question is who chooses it and whether the choice has to be reviewed and approved.

When looking at specific decision-making situations, first ask if it needs to be made at that level. Can it be made at the operational level? The objective is to totally *eliminate* the decision-making process. That is the way to lower the pyramid and empower people! If it is not possible to eliminate the entire decision-making process, then break the process down into its fundamental steps. No doubt at least some of these steps can be carried without any managerial involvement.

If and only if it is impossible to eliminate a complete decision process, then try to eliminate each step in the decision-making process. Failing that, try to at least *simplify* the process or any step within the decision-making process. As a last step, try to *combine* decision-making steps. As you do this, you streamline the organization and eliminate the need for vertical decision making. A graphical tool like the flow chart seen in figure 8–1 could be used to help one plot the steps, visualize the process, and focus on improvements and changes. The steps for this are seen below. Obviously, the more decision steps in operation that you eliminate, the easier it is to flatten the power pyramid (which is usually based on decision-making authority). The following is a step-by-step process for eliminating, simplifying, and combining (ESC) decisions.

ESC Steps
Decision Making
Step-by-Step Process

Step 1   Observe and understand current decision-making process.
Step 2   Document decisions by using a flow chart. (This would involve writing a detailed description of the decision-making process to be studied, listing every individual decision [or non-decision] that is made as well as how one gets from one decision point to the next.) An example of one flow chart is seen in figure 8–1.
Step 3   The key is to critically evaluate each step of the current decision-making process and any proposed changes in it. (This is where creativity and persistence pays off. Consider layout, organizational structure, and training, among other options, as ways of eliminating simplifying or combining steps.)
Step 4   Implement the change. (Ideas are important, but they will not help until they are implemented. Someone has to have patience and persistence to specify what is to be done, to assign responsibilities, and to follow up to see that instructions have been carried out.
Step 5   After sufficient time has passed, revise the decision-making steps when and as necessary.

Expert Systems

To look at how we might eliminate the need to make decisions, we need look no further than the use of computer technology; particularly one type of program called an "Expert System." Expert systems can be used to help automate the decision-making process so that only exceptional decision making (opportunities or crises) need human intervention. It might be noted that DuPont has already taken significant steps in this direction. In fact, they expect to have two thousand expert systems operational in 1991.

FLOW PROCESS CHART — NUMBER | PAGE NO. | NO. OF PAGES

PROCESS: Loan Application Processing
☐ MAN OR   ☐ MATERIAL

SUMMARY

ACTIONS	PRESENT		PROPOSED		DIFFERENCE	
	NO.	TIME	NO.	TIME	NO.	TIME
○ OPERATIONS						
◇ TRANSPORTATIONS						
☐ INSPECTIONS						
○ DELAYS						
▽ STORAGES						
DISTANCE TRAVELLED (FOOD)						

CHART BEGINS: Asst Scty's Desk (1)
CHART ENDS: File (15)
CHARTED BY: Donald Williams
DATE: 6/28/82
ORGANIZATION: Bank Branch Office

DETAILS OF ☐ PRESENT ☐ PROPOSED METHOD

Columns: OPERATIONS, TRANSPORTATIONS, INSPECTION, DELAYS, STORAGES, DISTANCE IN FEET, QUANTITY, TIME, ANALYSIS WHY? (WHAT? WHERE? WHEN? WHO? HOW?), NOTES, ANALYSIS (ELIMINATE, SIMPLIFY, COMBINE)

1. Assistant Secretary at her desk
2. She moves to Thermo-Fax Machine in back room.
3. Removes application from Thermo-Fax Machine.
4. Transports application to Manager's desk.
5. Secretary returns to her desk.
6. Application on Mgr's desk pending review.
7. Manager reviews the loan application.
8. Mgr transports application to Asst Mgr's desk.
9. Application on Asst Mgr's desk pending work-up.
10. Asst Mgr completes work-up of credit check.
11. Asst Mgr transports application to Mgr's desk.
12. Application on Mgr's desk pending approval/disapproval.
13. Manager approves/disapproves application.
14. Manager transports application to file.
15. Files application in the Pending File.

Figure 8–1. Charting the Flow of Work

They also expect to realize a 10 percent increase in profits from these systems. [1]

A great deal of decision making involves searching for information about how to resolve problems. Better problem definition and data collection could make significant improvements in this process. Even the selecting of alternatives and managerial control can be fairly automatic, and could be taken over by expert systems, artificial intelligence, or other technology.

Expert systems are a form of artificial intelligence based on software programs that have unique decision-making abilities. While most computer programs use algorithms in a step-by-step process to solve problems, expert systems are designed to make informed decisions just like people. For those unfamiliar with expert systems, remember those computer chess games that challenged even the best human chess experts? Some of those were toy expert systems. Today they are no longer a toy. Many of the businesses using expert systems are reporting a return on investment of as much as 1,000 percent.[2]

Expert systems can be customized to do specific tasks or arrive at the best solution to a specific problem. To create an expert system, you must have a knowledge base to draw from and a system of procedures for making decisions called an "inference engine." This inference engine examines the knowledge base to arrive at a desired solution.

Knowledge bases of expert systems are created by collecting information from human experts in a particular field. Expert systems take all the knowledge available in a specific area and then a designer of these systems builds thousands of *if/then* statements. These statements revolve around a series of situations (*if* statements) as well as possible responses to these situations (*then* statements). A manager using an expert system could then type in a situation (*if* statement) and receive an analysis of the problem and recommended solutions.

Expert systems can be created to resolve specific problems in areas such as maintenance, production, inventory, and purchasing. Expert systems could be used to classify safety problems and to suggest the best approach for eliminating a hazard. These systems can be used to troubleshoot breakdowns. Bell Labs in Fort Worth, Texas, uses a system called Automated Cable Expertise (ACE) to evaluate hundreds of thousands of cable repair reports each day. It decides when repairs are needed and suggests preventive maintenance so those problems can be avoided. General Electric developed DELAT (Diesel-Electric Locomotive Troubleshooting Aid) to help them repair diesels and electric locomotives.[3]

If you think such systems are only for the shop-floor level, think again. Palladian Software, Inc., of Cambridge, Massachusetts, has an expert system called Operations Advisor. It can be used for high-level planning. A vice-president of manufacturing could use it to evaluate cost impacts of changing production volume. Plant managers could use it to determine the plant capacity needed to obtain a specific lead time. Determining the best lot sizes or assessing the impact of purchasing new equipment are also within its domain.

There is a prototype knowledge-based system called Loan Evaluation Expert (LEE) that assists loan officers in assessing commercial loan applications, and this is despite the fact that loan application is one of the most challenging problem-solving situations faced by experienced bankers.[4]

Even strategic decisions are fertile grounds for expert systems. Arthur

D. Little, Inc., has developed several manufacturing, finance, and other business applications. A factory-layout expert system can assist in identifying and testing alternative layouts for product flows.

This is not as far as expert systems can or will go. In 1990, Ford Motor Company, Digital Equipment Corp., Texas Instruments, and U.S. West, Inc., agreed to cooperate in a crash effort known as "Initiative For Managing Knowledge Assets." The purpose of the program is to develop a standard for the building of expert systems. The group is hoping to overcome a fundamental problem with these systems—their inability to share information. Imagine the power these systems will have when they can interact with one another. It would be a powerful tool that could be used to automate higher-level managerial decisions as well as expert or staff functions.

The whole area of expert systems and decision-making technology is in rapid transition. One of the newer concepts is "Fuzzy Logic." Fuzzy logic is designed to operate around concepts of "maybe" rather than the definite "yes or no" decisions of digital logic. The result is sure to be greater capabilities and corresponding changes in organizational structure.

Streamlining the decision making so horizontal management can be implemented will no doubt involve the application of computers, but it is not the only way. Communication technology can establish procedures to automate the planning, searching, selecting, inspecting, and even controlling aspects of management. In quality control today, there is a strong push to eliminate staff inspections altogether and push decision making down to the operational level. Many are questioning the need for excessive controls or approvals so common in vertical organizations. Some specific organizations are eliminating, simplifying, or combining decision steps to evolve toward a more horizontal structure.

Computerized Networks

So far in this chapter and earlier in Chapter 6, I refer to the potential of computer technology as a means of achieving a more horizontal structure. One initial component of this computerized network may have already been developed by Globe Metallurgical Incorporated. Globe is a major producer of silicon and ferrosilicon products. The company is noted for outstanding quality, and in 1988 they were one of the first three winners of the United States's Malcolm Baldridge Quality Award. Globe began to focus on quality in 1985 when Ford Motor Company approached its suppliers, of which Globe was one, with Ford's quality certification program called Q-1.

Globe, seeking to enhance its relationship with Ford, instituted their own quality-improvement program by training their entire work force in statistical quality control, developing a quality manual, and educating their own suppliers on the value of quality. Concurrently, while Globe was upgrading their quality, their customers were demanding documentation of their quality. To do this Globe started using an evaluation tool known as process capability or Cpk.

Essentially, any operation has a certain amount of "inherent capability." This is the normal variation that can be expected to occur with plus or minus three sigma. Process capability, or Cpk, is simply the ability of a business to meet the customers' needs by producing a product that stays within this natural or inherent capability. Customers will often define what they want, for example a three-inch pipe, then set upper and lower tolerances. In this case, a customer might want a three-inch pipe, but would be willing to accept a $\pm.015$ of an inch tolerance.

For a business to calculate its process capability, they would take the upper limit minus the lower limit, (in this case it would be .030) and divide it by the process's natural inherent capability. If this inherent capability is less than .030, the number will be greater than 1.00. For instance, .030 divided by .010 equals 3.00. A value of 1.00 indicates the process exactly meets the total tolerance allowed by the customer. A value of less than 1.00 means the process is incapable of meeting the customer's specifications. A value greater than 1.00 means the process fits within the customer's needs. This is the best case. The higher the Cpk number, the more easily it fits within the customer's specifications.

Before 1986, Globe had fairly typical quality control, with generic production-control methods, and customers demanding 100 percent inspections of the goods bought from Globe. Using their production methods, their Cpk statistics were generally less than 1.0, which meant they were not meeting customer expectations. To improve the quality of their process, Globe developed a computerized system that allowed for the *customerization* of each product produced for each customer's different specifications and requirements.

In order to do this, they established a direct link between the IBM personal computer on the shop floor and their laboratory where molten samples are analyzed. In order to streamline the decision-making process by eliminating and simplifying unnecessary steps, hourly employees operated the system themselves; the computer calculated the ladle additive requirements for each batch and then employees made the ladle addition.[5]

Globe noted that in the production of magnesium ferrosilicon products there were many different chemical elements and distributions involved in the process. Customization in the process was impossible before the computerized system. Thanks to this system they could tailor end products. The result was very high Cpk, greater than 2.0 in most cases, and in many as high as 10.0. Because of this high quality, most of their customers relaxed the 100 percent inspection requirement.

Such computerized links between the shop floor and higher-level management activities are increasingly common. It is a natural progression to develop several such networks. While such systems may not be aimed at creating greater empowerment, they usually do result in responsibility, authority, and autonomy being shifted downward. In this case, the computer simplified the decision-making process enough that operational personnel could make decisions directly rather than having to wait on guidance from middle managers or staff.

Automation

Using computers to simplify the decision-making process enough so it can be delegated to the operational level was also General Electric's experience. In the 1980s, their circuit-breaker business was in a slow-growth mode and facing tough competition. This crisis forced G.E. to overhaul their manufacturing process. G.E. set a goal of cutting the throughput (the time between the customer order and delivery of the order) from three weeks to three days. Toward this end, they automated, made more parts interchangeable, and made managerial decision-making changes that brought about long-lasting corporate structural changes.

As part of this process, they developed a way to replace some of their staff and their engineers with a computer. "Now salespeople enter specifications for a circuit breaker into a computer at G.E.'s main office in Connecticut and the order flows to a computer in Salisburg, which automatically programs the factory machines to make circuit breakers with minimum waste of materials."[6]

Computerized networks that eliminate staff and middle managers are not the only way to simplify decision making so horizontal management would be easier to implement. DuPont needed to get leaner and more competitive, so they initiated their Early Retirement Opportunity (ERO) Program where over 11,000 employees left the company. From 1982 to 1986 other reductions occurred so that there was a total reduction in the workforce of about 29,000. The company had to figure out how to get their work completed with significantly fewer people.

Their human-resource people faced the same problem. They had reduced their staff, but also had to deal with ever-expanding human-resource issues, such as child care, parental leave, dual-career families, flexible benefits, and health concerns such as AIDS and drug testing, among other issues.

To deal with the downsizing they began assessing and prioritizing their work, as well as defining their strengths and weaknesses. From strategic meetings they developed a mission statement for the company. Later, departments developed their own statements to match the corporate objectives. The human-resources area also developed some major initiatives to manage better with less people. These initiatives included: (1) consolidating the human resource organization, (2) adding value through technology, (3) eliminating tasks, and (4) encouraging human resource employees to expand their roles and contributions.[7]

These initiatives helped guide the human-resource area to focus on *automation* of many human-resource activities. In particular, this involved the use of computer and video display equipment. Their corporate offices have a small group of Affirmative Action experts who worked with various plants. Rather than travel to each of these plants to work through a particular problem, their experts have prepared videotapes. The tapes are used by plant personnel when faced with routine, fairly automatic equal opportunity audits.

Plant managers can pull out a videotape that shows the systematic step-by-step preparation process. If there are special questions or information that is needed along the way, they can always call the corporate human-resource consultants. Since both plant managers and corporate people are working from the same data base, communication links are improved.

Such preprogrammed instructions bring the automatic corporate stage one step closer to reality. DuPont does not expect to stop at Affirmative Action. They see many other applications whenever the responses needed are predictable and repetitive, such as OSHA inspections, training activities, and benefits consultation.

In an effort to automate repetitive activities, they have an automated touch-tone phone system to handle the more routine calls from pensioners. The pensioner dials a recording that provides specific information on such matters as how to fill out dental or medical forms or when the next pension check will be mailed out. Additionally, DuPont uses a computerized service manual so changes can be made electronically, eliminating the need to render updates. As one might expect, they also make extensive use of electronic mail.

Eliminating and simplifying decision making is a better choice, but combining procedures and decision making can also be used to implement horizontal management and improve competitiveness. DuPont does this by encouraging people to assume greater responsibility. Rather than having their professional drivers spend their spare time polishing cars, they now spend it teaching defensive driving to other employees during nondriving hours. This is an excellent example of delegating a task to the operational level rather than leaving it to a staff person. Toward the same end, DuPont notes that human-resource leaders will get ahead by being generalists. They will spend more of their time working on committees and special projects where they are exposed to others.

Approvals

Technology is not the only way to reduce the hierarchy. Successive layers of management often tend to develop because of the distrust inherent to most vertical organizations. This distrust shows up in many ways, but the most common is the internal approval process that exists in most organizations. Internal approvals add vertical height quicker than just about any other activity. Simple flow charts, where you plot out the step-by-step decision-making process, soon reveal bottlenecks, backtracking, and excessive waste as jobs are delayed because of the organizational internal-approval process.

As noted in Chapter 2, Jack Reichert, CEO of Brunswick, the $3 billion sporting goods company, cut the layers of management between himself and the shop workers from ten to five. "If you want to know how to do a job right, ask the people who are doing it; don't have some bureaucracy tell them how to do it."[8] As mentioned earlier, he increased spending authority for division heads from $25,000 to $250,000. That eliminated a lot of decisions. At his headquarters in Illinois, he only gets a weekly one-page report from each division chief. He says the reports "tell me what they need."

Adca Bank, a subsidiary of Germany's Rabo Bank, used a loan process similar to that of most other banks. Applications went through layers of bureaucracy. Branches sent loan papers to headquarters where they were either approved or not. Adca's solution was to get rid of five layers of management by giving all branches more authority. Before, it took twenty-four man-hours to approve a loan; now it takes twelve.

Work Out

Perhaps one of the organizations with the keenest interest in streamlining by eliminating decision making, redundancy, and other unnecessary work is General Electric. G.E. is more than one company. It consists of thirteen distinct businesses and including producers of aircraft engines, medical systems, engineering plastics, and major appliances, several financial institutions, and NBC television. In 1989 its almost 300,000 employees generated $55 billion in revenues and had a net income of $4 billion. Most of their business divisions rank first or second in the world.

They have been very profitable, but it did not come easily. In part, it came about through massive "de-layering." From 1980 to 1985, John F. Welch, Jr., the chairman and CEO of G.E., trimmed the payroll from 410,000 to 291,000.

To understand their success, you must first understand where they started. In 1980, many of G.E.'s divisions had as many as nine layers of management. By 1990, all of their businesses' layers of management have been significantly reduced; some have as few as four or five levels.

Welch took over the helm of G.E. from Reginald H. Jones. Under Jones, a finance man, "G.E. went from a chronic state of cash shortage to immense financial strength. Jones also built up the bureaucracy, adding more complex financial reporting to the military-style command-and-control system. The new reports collected vast amounts of data—'I found you never get all the information you'd like,' Jones recalls—and forced decisions through thickets of reviews."[9] The result was that the bureaucracy overwhelmed top executives.

Welch, the engineer, made changes, stating that, "If we put bureaucracy and rigidness into our system, we play into our competitors' hands in global markets."[10] G.E.'s current CEO regards bureaucracy as an evil. It is rigid; it resists change. He believes it makes people look inward at the organization, not outward as they should toward their customers and the competition.

During his tenure, Welch has been driven to identify and eliminate unproductive work. He knows that expecting employees to do volumes of reviews, budgets, and reports is unrealistic. The work itself has to change. He knows that "for a large organization to be effective, it must be simple. For a large organization to be simple, its people must have self confidence and intellectual self-assurance. Insecure managers produce complexity."[11] They produce approvals, checks and double checks, procedures, rules and regulations, reports, and reviews.

To turn this attitude around requires that the corporate office change its attitude. It requires a small rather than a large staff. The corporate staff no longer just challenges and questions, it assists the field. As Welch noted, "Staff essentially reports to the field rather than the other way around."[12]

Work Out is one of the key processes that Welch is using at G.E. to improve competitiveness. The objective is to eliminate the thousands of bad habits that tend to build up over time. G.E. is 112 years old, so there is a high probability that many inefficiencies have been built into their organization's structure.

Work Out begins with a series of regularly scheduled "town meetings" involving a large cross section of a business. It is estimated that 20,000 to 25,000 employees from manufacturing, engineering, and customer service attend these work sessions each year. Both hourly and salaried employees participate. They meet with the heads of the thirteen main business units in G.E.

Individuals in these groups are picked from all levels and are usually chosen because of their expertise and involvement in a particular issue. The purpose is to get divergent viewpoints and, through discussion, to agree to eliminate or simplify the more bureaucratic aspects of an organization. Some of the focus in the past has been on eliminating multiple approvals, unnecessary paperwork, excessive red tape, reports, routines, rituals, and other unnecessary tasks.

Because the leader is expected to take action on the results of the discussion, follow-up meetings are also held. In initial meetings he or she listens to the group's ideas for half the day, then for the rest of the day the leader goes through each idea identifying ones that can be corrected immediately and ones that will need further study. It is during the follow-up meetings that those needing further study are addressed. Once Work Out sessions eliminate the obvious bureaucratic problems, the focus turns more toward a detailed analysis of the production process, identifying the critical few steps in the process and discarding the trivial many.

An example of using Work Out sessions involved their medical-supplies business's X-ray unit near Milwaukee. The session identified fifty-five items that could be eliminated or simplified. In one case, the group determined that the head of their computing lab should be able to spend petty cash and sign for approvals without permission of a supervisor. Another similar session spotlighted the fact that one thousand people worked nights and weekends at the end of each quarter so G.E. could have the honor of being the first company its size to publicly report earnings. What they discovered was that no one cared, so they eliminated the work.

It is always amazing to see what becomes built into a system. Programs like Work Out, when properly administered, produce simple structures focused on speed and efficiency.

Concluding Thoughts

How far this streamlining process can go is anyone's guess. My own feeling is that this eliminating, simplifying, and combining of processes has infinite potential. Incremental improvements in the decision-making process are possible because there is always a way to streamline. In a world where constant change is the only constant that exists, change is essential.

Notes

1. D. Keith Denton, "Decision-Making Technology," *P&IM Review* 8, no. 1 (January 1988), p. 35.

2. Ibid., p. 35.

3. Ibid.

4. Angelo G. Brovos, "LEE: Loan Evaluation Expert, A Prototype Expert System for the Assessment of Loan Applications," in *ESD/SMI Expert System Conference and Exposition for Advanced Manufacturing Technology*, Dearborn, Michigan, 9–11 June 1987, p. 394.

5. Kenneth E. Leach, "The Development of the Globe Metallurgical Quality System", In-house publication.

6. Brian Dumaine, "How Managers Can Succeed Through Speed," *Fortune,* 13 February 1989, p. 56.

7. H. Gordon Smyth, "Is There Life After Restructuring? DuPont's Experience With Downsizing the Human Resource," *Conference Board Annual Resources Conference,* New York, 11 October 1988. p. 3.

8. Dumaine, p. 3.

9. Stratford Sherman, "Inside the Mind of Jack Welch," *Fortune,* 27 March, 1989, p. 38.

10. Ibid., p. 38.

11. Tichy Noel and Ram Charan, "Speed, Simplicity, Self Confidence: An Interview With Jack Welch," *Harvard Business Review* September–October 1989, pp. 114.

12. Ibid., p. 114.

9
Teams

MIT's Productivity Commission chairman, Michael L. Dertouzos, notes, "Organizing for innovation means flattening the hierarchy, giving more responsibility to the lower levels, scuttling discipline-oriented departments in favor of ad hoc mission team groups." Forget the organizational structure we have used for three hundred years, says Robert L. Callahan, president of Ingersoll Engineers, Inc. Simply put together people who can get the job done, regardless of their function.[1] Regardless of what you call it, there is little doubt that teams—all degrees, all levels, and all kinds of teams—will be a key component to any new emerging horizontal management structure.

Types of Teams

Teams come in all shapes, sizes and dispositions. As a tool, they can be used at the lowest or highest level within the organization. Ford Motor Company's use of them provides an excellent example of the wide range of teams available to management.

Perhaps the most common type of team, and one used by Ford, is the *problem-solving team*, sometimes called a department team. It is usually an immediate work group dealing with its own job-related issues such as quality, productivity, or cost problems.

Special-project teams, or simply project teams, are usually created around special issues or events. They focus on process improvement or what Ford refers to as concept-to-customer or "total customer satisfaction" objectives. These teams are often used for crisis situations. They can be very broad in nature or very narrowly focused on a specific situation.

Opportunity teams at Ford are formed on an ad hoc basis. They are often formed because of upcoming work-related changes. These might include changes in company policy, procedures, and regulations. Introducing a new policy to hire the handicapped or another disadvantaged group might be enhanced by using opportunity teams to evaluate the potential and challenges.

Linking teams, sometimes called interdepartmental teams, usually include individuals from other teams. This kind of team is formed when there is a need for interdepartmental, intershift or cross-functional coordination. Such teams are usually created to coordinate production, process, and design considerations. TQM, where the emphasis is on getting all functional areas involved in implementing customer satisfaction, might be one example where linking teams could be beneficial.

Ford and other organizations are making more of use of teams that include members outside the organizational structure. Ford calls theirs the *Vendor, Dealer, and Customer Quality* team. As the name implies, Ford uses the team to meet with their vendors, dealers, and customers to develop solutions to problems, prevent problems from occurring, or as a way to seek new opportunities.

Many line-staff teams are created to reduce the lateral misunderstandings and communication problems typical of vertical organization. *Cross-functional* teams are created to work on complex issues requiring a broad range of knowledge and experience not found on any one level. A need for such a team might arise when dealing with strategic or financial issues. Later in the book, we look at how a Rohm and Haas Bayport, Inc., plant makes use of this approach.

A *hybrid team* is any combination of the above teams.

Teams in Context

Horizontal Network Teams

Teams can and logically should be classified not only by their type, but by the context in which they are used. Teams can be used as an auxiliary or supplemental means of improving cross-functional and interdepartmental communication and cooperation. In these cases, the actual vertical organization structure, with its corresponding lines of authority, has not changed. Teams are essentially add-on techniques designed to help compensate for the inherent deficiencies and difficulties of pyramid organizations. These *horizontal network teams* can improve the flow of information through knotted lines of communication and enhance the creative energy of traditional vertical organizations. A company that knows the power of such teams is the one discussed in Chapter 8, Globe Metallurgical.

Globe is renowned for their quality and customer-satisfaction efforts. It uses a fairly typical vertical structure. Their use of team management to supplement normal lines of authority is a primary reason why Globe has been so successful.

In the mid 1980s, Globe's quality efforts were not what they are today. Their hourly employees' ideas for quality and productivity were not solicited. Lack of attention to their employees' needs led to frequent labor problems. In 1986, realizing that things would have to change if they were to remain competitive, they created quality-circle teams at each of Globe's plants.

One of their quality-circle teams was called the *departmental team*. Each of these teams were composed of approximately seven hourly employees from within one specific department. Team members met weekly to discuss improvements in their department. Employees met either before or after their shift and were paid overtime for these meetings, which usually lasted about one hour.

Meetings were chaired by the team leader who was an hourly employee in the group. These leaders were trained to keep the team focused on improved quality, efficiency, and cost. Ideas were solicited from each member and written on a pre-printed form. On average, about ten ideas were generated from each meeting.

Their particular style of team decision making was an almost pure example of step 1 horizontal problem solving (see figure 6–1). The work group perspective was narrowly focused strictly on problem investigation and recommendation. Higher-level decision making was reserved for the higher-ups. Thus, upper management was still responsible for problem identification as well as for actual selection from those recommendations made by those employees on the departmental teams.

When employee team members develop proposals and ideas, they are passed on to the Coordinator for Quality Circles, who is a salaried (management) employee. This individual sits on the Quality Efficiency Cost (QEC) Committee, which consists of management personnel. This is the decision-making group at each plant.

In addition to the QEC committee is the QEC Steering Committee, which oversees the activities of each of these plant committees. The Steering Committee is composed of the top officials of the company, and is chaired by the president and the CEO. This group meets monthly and discusses the broader strategic issues of developing and maintaining the quality system at Globe. Issues discussed usually relate to allocation of resources and planning.

The plant QEC committee meets daily. It is chaired by the plant manager and is attended by department heads. The link between this plant QEC committee and the QEC Steering Committee is the plant manager. He is the conduit between corporate directives and their implementation at the plant level.

This QEC committee discusses and makes the more narrowly focused decisions concerning specific projects and ways to implement the decisions. This includes deciding what should and should not be controlled and how it will be controlled. For example, the QEC plant committee could decide to solve a particular quality problem and decide to use SPC to do it.

Within this traditional vertical organization, there are basically three levels of decision making. Departmental teams are at the bottom of the decision-making pyramid. These teams are composed of hourly employees that meet weekly to discuss ways to improve performance. Their efforts are primarily focused on step 1 (figure 6–1) of the Horizontal Management Continuum.

Actual problem resolution and decision making is performed by the plant QEC committee. The plant manager, as chair of the QEC committee, has extensive authority to implement ideas without further approval. At these meetings ideas are read aloud, and the QEC committee either makes an immediate recommendation or holds for further review. Disposition of each item is written down on the form that ideas were turned in on and posted in a designated area of the plant. As they return for their next shift following the meeting, employees can immediately know the outcome of their ideas.[2]

Globe's quality decision making is essentially a horizontal network rather than a change in the structure of decision making. They did not reduce or change their relationship or lines of authority. Instead, they wove horizontal decision making throughout the corporation. While they did not change the organizational structure, Globe did try to insure that all levels had a chance to participate. They even gave employees a chance for input into their higher-level decision-resolution stages. Copies of their quality plans and goals created by the QEC Steering Committee are distributed, and hourly employees are invited to attend plant QEC committee planning meetings.

Additionally, Globe used *interdepartmental* or linking teams in order to add more horizontal flow within the organization. All the members of a linking team are hourly employees. The administrative process was the same as for the departmental teams; the only difference was that departmental interaction was necessary. The objective was to try to eliminate problems that have historically existed between departments.

Special project teams were also used on an ad hoc basis to tackle specific problems or projects. These teams, unlike departmental or interdepartmental teams, made use of salaried employees as well as hourly employees. Salaried employees sit on the teams because of their unique expertise. This includes knowledge of problem-solving techniques such as "Taguchi design experiments, storyboarding brainstorming techniques, and other advanced statistical techniques."[3]

While the lines of authority and structure at Globe remain the same, their network of teams have helped to get greater input from lower levels. Before the change in leadership style, only Globe's salaried employees did the same thing that project teams now do. Today over 60 percent of Globe's work force is involved in their team approach.[4]

Horizontal Structure Teams

As the previous discussion shows, horizontal network teams provide improved communication and motivation among vertical organization members. However, this is not the limit of what teams can do. They can even be used to change the very structure of an organization. Rather than augmenting the normal lines of authority, they can be used to change decision-making authority itself. In some cases, these teams have participated with management in joint decision making; in other cases, the use of teams has resulted in the redistribution of authority and accountability.

Network teams focus primarily on problem identification and investigation. As you recall, Globe's plant manager still had the ultimate responsibility and authority. While network teams concentrate on problem identification and investigation, structural teams do this *and* focus on problem resolution as well. The actual making of decisions, rather than simply having input into decision making, is the key difference between network and structural teams. In network teams, decision-making power is still sharply divided along lines of authority. With structural teams, this power is no longer compartmentalized; no one group has the ultimate power. At the very least, it is shared equally among organizational members.

An example of this type of arrangement is in the area of product development, which you might recall from the Horizontal Management Continuum, is a step V type of decision. Traditionally, product and process management has operated separately, connected only by lines of authority. Recently, this relationship has been changing in some of the more progressive companies. Rather than production personnel or process designers taking precedent, they have been combined to form a different type of decision-making process.

AT&T provides us with one example of how this transformation is occurring. When AT&T began developing their new 4200 cordless phone, John Hanley, AT&T's vice-president of Product Development, knew they needed to get to the market sooner. Barriers existed everywhere. He faced the typical rigid vertical bureaucracy. He said in the past AT&T's product development, "worked like a relay race, with the engineering department handing a design over to manufacturing, which handed the finished product over to marketing to sell."[5]

For their 4200 model, they decided to form teams of six to twelve members that included engineers, manufacturers, and marketers with the *authority to make every decision* on how the product would work, look, be made, and cost. They had six weeks to freeze all designs. Since they did not have to send each decision up the line for approval, they were able to meet that deadline. This new decision-making arrangement cut development time from two years to one year, while lowering costs and improving quality.

The microprocessor manufacturer, Intel Corporation, faced the same problems as AT&T. Moving fast and creating better designs was the key to success in their business. To pack their 386 chips with the computing power of a mainframe, they would need to develop new technology. However, "tinkering with a novel production at the same time the chip was being created raised the worrisome prospect of a geometric increase in problems that inevitably bedevil new products."[6]

To better manage their product development, they set up teams for their specialties and held weekly GYAT (Get Your Act Together) meetings where engineers and designers simply ironed out problems as they occurred. The process worked so well that Intel began applying the same approach to their other products. So what were the results? Four years ago it used to take sixty-four weeks to take a simple new chip from concept to profitability. With this new team approach, they set a goal of fifty-two weeks, and one team group of the 386 family did it in forty-eight weeks.

The horizontal structural team concept has application far beyond process and production research and development. Merck and Company, one of the best managed and most creative innovators in the medical field, takes the product development team concept even further. The company assigns a team leader for each research effort. The leader, acting as a conduit, must then guide the product through the entire process from basic research to final governmental approval.[7]

IBM is getting into team management in a big way at their world-renowned, highly automated typewriter assembly plant in Lexington, Kentucky. The plant's high degree of advanced assembly is an important factor in their success, but automation is not the whole story. Management notes that the most crucial changes came in their white-collar area and in the way the company designs and manufactures the one million typewriters and printers that Lexington ships each year.[8]

The key to their success is that every new product is shepherded by a manager who oversees both the design and manufacture. This person is assisted by an engineering team drawn from the plant's various departments. Among other considerations, the team even makes sure that the product is designed for highly automated production.[9] This is definitely an improvement over the days when designs were "tossed over the wall" from one department to another.[9]

IBM's use of this joint coordination and decision making is not unique. This type of cooperation between product and production, using interdepartmental teams, is becoming very popular. There is even an engineering term for it. It is called *concurrent* engineering. As the name implies, it involves the simultaneous development of both production and the product design to make a producible and profitable product. "The factory types do their thing even as the product is taking shape. Northrop Corporation is even giving manufacturing engineers veto power over designs."[10] Ford

Motor Company is a big proponent too. John P. McTague, vice-president of Research at Ford, says, "The more design and production become seamless, the better [off] we'll be."[11]

Teamwork

General Electric's (G.E.) extensive experience with managing teams has given it insight into what it takes to make one work. Linda Brooks is a relations specialist for G.E. and a "coach" for one of their teams at G.E.'s appliance facility in Decatur, Alabama. Their main assembly line of ninety workers was divided into teams. Members on each team rotated so everyone would know all the jobs on the team. Preparation and training for effective teams actually began long before this cross-training effort.

Before people are hired, they attend pre-hire classes for seven weeks, three hours a day, two days a week. In these meetings they discuss things like the effects of competition, quality, and productivity. It is at this early stage that they first begin to focus on teamwork.

Brooks explains that their efforts involve groups going through a team-building exercise. "We set up assembly lines for making paper airplanes. Each person makes a fold and passes it on. People can't talk to each other. At the end, the planes are flight tested. As you can imagine, many don't fly. Then we do it again. This time they can talk to each other. The planes fly."[12]

If team management is going to become a larger part of management, training must be effective. Simply forming a project task force is not enough. As G.E. recognizes, it takes teamwork to produce effective teams.

Enrique Sosa, a group vice-president for Dow Chemical, made the point that he had been on many teams and that effective ones have a certain philosophy. They practice the art of *compromise* in order to reach a goal, always keeping in mind that no one team member can know all the variables involved in complex situations and that the external customer must be kept in mind when making decisions.

Bethlehem Steel provides us with an excellent example of a special-projects team that was successful in part because it used *team goals*. In 1988 Bethlehem wanted to improve their delivery performance. Their on-time shipments were running about 50 percent. By 1989 (one year later), this number had been turned around. Instead of 50 percent, it was running about 85 percent, and in some cases it had improved to over 90 percent.

To improve on-time shipping, a team of employees from their steel operations, as well as others from production services, product offices, and field sales, were brought together to look at delivery through the *eyes of the customer*. Their goal was to improve sales promises to the customer and their own compliance to production schedules. They concentrated on three areas: (1) the percentage of items ready on time versus the original acknowledged date given to the customer, (2) their scheduled compliance in terms of actual on-time shipment versus their final expected-to-be-shipped date, and (3) overall performance in terms of items not shipped as promised.

Their improvement in performance and in the performance of the team was not due to drastic changes in their operation in order-entry functions. Rather, it was that they focused on the *customer's perception of service.*[13] This gave them a goal around which to center all their activities. With a clear goal, they were able to gather information on previous delivery data, to establish control limits, and to improve manufacturing lead times and standards as well as find out what their competition was doing.

Team goals were essential for success and good group decision making. Ford, for one, believes that without shared goals, group decision making is a waste of time because little will be accomplished. When creating teams, first ask yourself, "Are your group's goals clear to all members?" "Is everyone trying to achieve the same thing?" "Does each person agree with the goals?" "Has each had a say in deciding the goals?" and "Are there too many goals?"[14]

Team Roles

In order to accomplish those goals, Ford also stresses that each member of a team needs to know what role each team member plays. After defining their roles, each member must be able to handle the responsibility assigned to him or her. Work should be evenly distributed among members with each having an equal chance to participate in assigning work.

Like Ford, Metropolitan Life Insurance Company (Met Life) believes that defining roles is vital to problem solving and team building. Met Life defines these roles in one of four categories. One of these roles is what they call the *client.* This team member is responsible for asking for assistance in solving a problem and "(1) decides what the meeting is about, (2) provides the group with relevant background information, (3) describes the problem clearly, (4) after brainstorming, selects the most promising roles for further evaluation, and (5) eventually completes an action plan."[15]

Teams also need someone to play the role of *facilitator.* The facilitator is responsible for keeping the meeting on track. He or she does this by keeping members focused on the problem, keeping them focused on time commitments, classifying ideas, remaining neutral, and making sure all the members' ideas are properly discussed.

Another key role is that of *recorder.* As the name implies, this member is responsible for taking notes (usually on a flip chart for everyone to see) so everyone can agree on the results of the discussion. Recorders make sure there is a uniform record of the group's efforts. He or she also serves the group because the recorder's efforts help everyone develop a better grasp of the key points of discussions. Usually, after group meetings, recorders are responsible for making sure the notes on the meeting are typed up and sent to team members.

The remaining members of the group play the role of *resources*. These members' responsibilities are to contribute ideas and communicate.

This brings up the last key point about interteam communication. Ford, along with Met Life, believes that relationships are essential for teamwork. Members of the team must cooperate with each other. They must work together and be able to resolve conflicts before they can really be a team. If members on the team do not communicate, do not listen, and are looking out for only themselves, then little can be expected. Just forming a team is not enough; members have to be trained to be members of teams. It takes special skills to make a team work.

A System for Teams

Most solutions begin with training, and team management is no exception. Training members of teams to be productive is exactly what Nissan Motor Company does with their teams. Nissan makes extensive use of teams they call "Involvement Circles." These circles are used by Nissan to involve employees in finding solutions to problems concerned with quality, safety, and productivity. At their plant located in Smyrna, Tennessee, they have fifty-five Involvement Circles in all seven divisions of the company, including ones for their administrative and production personnel. Circles are voluntary and average ten members. They meet weekly during work hours or are paid overtime to come in after work.

Nissan's circle leaders and team facilitators receive twenty hours of training in the problem-solving process, listening skills, conducting effective meetings, and team building. The corporation also enhances the linkages with their teams by having their maintenance, engineering, human resources, finance, and purchasing departments receive special training to familiarize themselves with their Involvement Circle process. The purpose is to improve the communication process, which is vital to team productivity.

Met Life's systematic training for their team management includes training on how to use a variety of these team communication techniques. Met Life believes it is interpersonal communication skills that help group members work together. Specific techniques they focus on include training members on how to use communication techniques like reflecting, paraphrasing, using open-ended questions, reacting with benefits before concerns, and headlining. An explanation of each of these communication techniques is seen in table 9–1.

As part of Met Life's team management approach, they teach each member the logical sequence of steps for arriving at solutions. These steps are summarized in table 9–2.

Table 9–1
Problem Solving/Team Building: Summary of Communication Techniques

Technique	What It Is
Reflecting:	Crystallizing what a person is saying to let him or her know you are connecting; it is generally used to mirror back to the speaker the emotion or feeling that you—as listener—are experiencing. *Example:* "You're really pleased about that."
Paraphrasing:	Restating what someone has just said to make sure that you have understood what was said. *Example:* "What I hear you saying . . ."; "It sounds like . . ."; "It seems like . . ."
Open-ended Questions:	Using questions phrased in such a way that they require more than a "yes" or "no" answer. They allow a person to open up and tell you more. They allow you to get more information, to clarify and to obtain feedback. These types of questions are formulated by using words like: *what, where, how* and *why.*
Reacting with Benefits before Concerns:	Looking at the strong points of an idea first, before looking at an idea's flaws. In other words, we look at the benefits of an idea before we express our concerns about it. This helps to nurture ideas and move past the acceptability threshold, where they become useful, viable ideas.

Table 9–1 continued

Technique	What It Is
Headlining:	Capsulizing an idea in a few succinct words before expanding on it. This signals to a listener where the speaker is headed and the point he or she wishes to make, so that the listener's attention is more focused.

Courtesy of Metropolitan Life Insurance Co.

Table 9–2
Problem Solving/Team Building: Summary of Sequence of Steps

Activity	Brief Description
Step 1: Defining current situation with background	State relevant facts and activities which help identify that a problem exists. Include prior actions or thoughts that have already been considered and define the results desired by using this problem solving process.
Step 2: Formulating the problem statement	Develop a concise action statement beginning with "How to," include an action verb that denotes accomplishment and state what we expect done and when we expect it. (How much? How soon?)
Step 3: Brainstorming	Open up the problem solving by developing thoughts, wishes, suggestions, and action recommendations on how to accomplish the objective identified.
Step 4: Selecting ideas	Select a single idea or group of ideas for further development. Sometimes, if all ideas are promising, the facilitator asks the client to prioritize them.

Table 9–2 continued	
Activity	**Brief Description**
Step 5: Analysing the benefits/ concerns	Develop a list of at least three benefits, before listing your concerns. Phrase concerns as potential problems in "How to" statements. For example, "How to get the resources we need to implement this idea."
Step 6: Overcoming concerns	Generate ideas to overcome any concerns that must be addressed before the selected idea can be implemented. In other words, recycle concerns through the sequence of steps as new problems, if necessary.
Step 7: Creating the action plan	Identify the "next steps," which will assure that the chosen idea becomes a solution to the problem. During the process the individual (or group) identifies next activities, assigns responsibilities, plans the sequence of activities, and sets up appropriate controls to monitor progress and communicate results.

Courtesy of Metropolitan Life Insurance Co.

Team Problem-solving Techniques

Setting up a communication system is vital to team success, but reaching a team's full potential depends on training members how to solve problems. Aluminum Company of America (ALCOA) provides us with an excellent case of an organization using a team problem-solving approach. Their process occurs within their Eight Step Quality Improvement Process. In essence, this eight-step process was based on W. Edward Deming's philosophy and principles of scientific management.

Deming stressed a simple plan-do-check-act-cycle. This involves first defining problems, selecting the problem (or opportunity) for further study, analyzing cause and effect, generating potential actions, evaluating those actions, testing the effectiveness of those actions, then implementing and monitoring.[16] ALCOA admits it is not essential that this process be followed step by step. It is intended to be flexible so it could be applied to almost any problem.

The heart of their eight-step process does involve using specific problem-solving techniques. ALCOA calls these techniques their seven quality tools. Their tools are descriptive statistical and graphical tools seen in figure 9–1. They did not invent these operational tools, but they have made excellent use of them.

These tools include the use of *check sheets* used to determine "how often certain things happen." It consists of simple hash marks placed be-

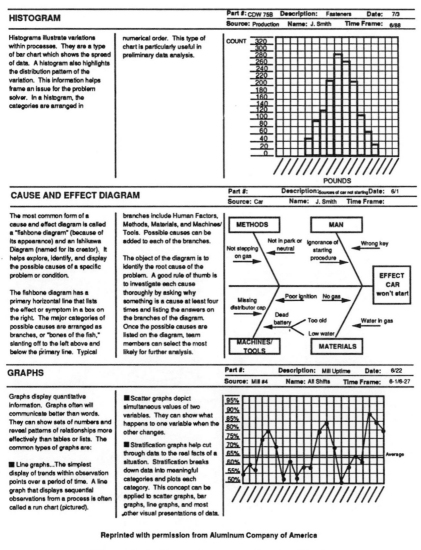

Reprinted with permission from Aluminum Company of America

Figure 9–1. Seven Common Quality Tools

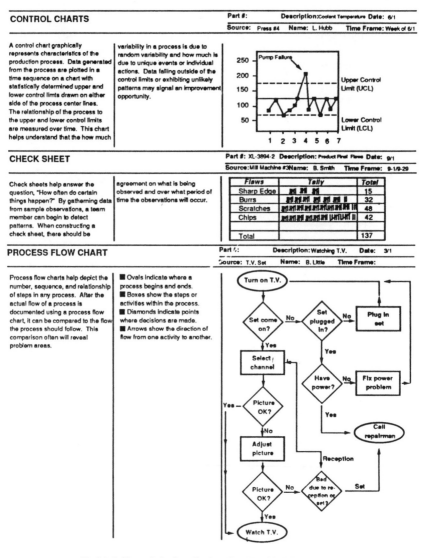

Reprinted with permission from Aluminum Company of America

Figure 9–1 (cont.)

side descriptions of typical occurrences or problems that are being investigated. This way the team can quickly begin to see where the most serious problems are occurring.

Once a team (or individual) has an idea of a problem that needs further investigation, the team can use a *process flow chart*. This chart shows the sequence of actions and decisions occurring and which ones are critical to resolving the situation.

PARETO CHART

Part #:   Description: Source of Computer Downtime   Date: 1/1

Source: Time Sharing System Name: R. Swanson   Time Frame: 9/1 - 12/31

Pareto charts identify the order or ranking among different factors influencing a problem. A form of vertical bar charts, Pareto charts can be used to point out a major problem or root cause. On the other hand, they also can be used to monitor success. Bars are arranged from the largest on the left to the smallest on the right. This focuses attention on the most important factors of an issue.

From the top of the tallest bar and moving upward from left to right, a line can be added that shows the cumulative frequency of each category measured on the chart.

This answers the question, "How much of the problem is accounted for by each category?" The Pareto principle states that it is common for 80 percent of the observations to be cause by only 20 percent of the causes. By concentrating on the "critical few," major improvement can be achieved by attacking a few causes.

Figure 9–1 (cont.)

A *Pareto chart* graphically helps a team rank the most significant factors affecting a problem or situation. These charts consist of vertical bars that highlight the "critical few" as well as the "trivial many." The bars are arranged from the most common, or taller bars, on the left to the smaller bars, or less frequent occurrences, on the right. As ALCOA notes, it answers the question, "How much of the problem is accounted for by each category?"

Use of the *histogram* or bar chart is another one of their seven tools. Like the Pareto chart, it graphically illustrates the distribution of occurrences and helps a team frame the problem and its causes.

ALCOA also makes use of the *cause and effect* or fish-bone diagram. This tool is usually used once a problem has been defined and isolated. Next, a team discovers what is causing the problem (or effect) such as poor quality in a specific area. In a cause-and-effect diagram, the horizontal line or axis is where the problem is listed. Possible reasons for this problem are listed on the slanted lines running away from the effect or problem (horizontal line). Primarily, the object of this tool is to identify root or basic causes of problems being investigated.

ALCOA's use of the seven tools also entails the use of other graphs and control charts. These include a variety of tools, such as line graphs, scatter graphs, and others, that help a team focus on a particular problem. Control charts, as noted in an earlier chapter, provide a means of measuring and monitoring a process after it is "in control." Once major problems have been investigated and solutions found, control charts are used by operators to monitor and record the results of operators' performance. It is both a motivational and a problem-solving tool because it provides feedback on what is occurring.

Problem Solving in Action

Not all of these tools need to be used in team problem-solving situations, but an understanding of how to use all of them should be available to all team members. An example of how such a problem-solving sequence might be used is provided by ALCOA's Jim Hanna. He was a production and control manager at an ALCOA plant and a member of one of their problem-solving teams. His team's objective was to improve the accuracy of their invoices. Management wanted to make sure invoices were showing the right prices for products and were actually delivered to customers.

In approaching their task, the team had to understand completely the order-entry and invoicing processes. "Each team member understood elements of the order-entry and invoicing processes, but only a few of us had been trained in the use of the quality tool," noted Jim Hanna.[17]

Initially, they constructed a simple flow chart, but each time they looked at the process they kept adding information about what was involved in the invoice process. Management Information Services provided information on the process, procurement added to their understanding, and the credit department also helped. In the end, their understanding as well as the complexity of their flow chart was greatly enhanced.

As a result of their analysis, they developed a comprehensive picture of what was involved. At that point they could then, and only then, begin the problem-solving process of collecting data to support probable cause and effect relationships. As time goes on, the team will use the problem-solving tools to evaluate, recommend, monitor, and make improvements.

Concluding Thoughts

Teams are going to be *the* primary management tool of the 1990s and beyond. They will be at the heart of efforts to empower employees and increase both an organization's effectiveness or competitiveness. Companies from A to Z are actively experimenting with the team-management concept. Hopefully, they will not use it in the piecemeal approach so common in American management.

Long-term success will depend on managers first sitting down together and deciding what they want to accomplish and then how far they want to take their empowerment efforts *before* they decide how to do it. Management must decide if they want to keep their old vertical organization in place and simply use horizontal network teams to try to improve the circulation of information and input.

On the other hand, management may feel, as I do, that there is a need to overhaul the structure of the organization in order to remain competitive. This does not necessarily mean radical restructuring. There are degrees of change. In fact, it is probably best in most cases to evolve from hierarchies to horizontals gradually. Structural decision-making teams can occur from step I through step V. It seems logical that coordinating these efforts would produce far better results than the random efforts that are typical of many organizations.

In the next two chapters, we will examine some of the options and opportunities for implementing team management. We can begin with one of the most powerful and popular means of changing structure at the operational level, namely Autonomous Small Work Groups. Later, we see how team management has gone far beyond this and is even being used in corporate strategic decision making.

Notes

1. Kenneth E. Leach, "The Development of the Globe Metallurgical Quality System," In-house publication, pp. 9.
2. Ibid,. p. 9.
3. Ibid., p. 10.
4. Ibid., p. 10.
5. Brian Dumaine, "How Managers Can Succeed Through Speed," *Fortune,* 13 February, 1989, pp. 52–57.
6. Richard Brandt, "It Takes More Than A Good Idea," in "Innovation in America," *Business Week,* 1989, p. 123.
7. Joseph Weber, "A Culture That Just Keeps Dishing Up Success," in "Innovation in America," *Business Week,* 1989, p. 120.
8. Zachary Schiller, "Big Blue's Big Overhaul," in "Innovation in America," *Business Week,* 1989, p. 147.
9. Ibid.
10. Otis Port, "A New Vision For the Factory," in "Innovation in America," *Business Week,* 1989, p. 146.
11. Ibid., p. 146.
12. Carol A. Dwyer, "Teamwork Pays Off," *Monogram* 68, no. 2 (Spring 1990), p. 16.
13. "On-Time Shipments: From Liability to Strategic Weapon," *Bethlehem Steel Review,* no. 2 (1989), pp. 8–9.
14. *Continuous Improvement Through Participation,* Education and Personnel Research Department, Ford Motor Company, 1984, p. 16.
15. *The Quality Improvement Process Personal Insurance, Field Edition-Employee Handbook,* Metropolitan Life Insurance Company, 1986, p. 13.
16. "Eight Steps To Quality Improvement," *ALCOA News,* March/April 1990, p. 13.
17. Ibid., p. 13.

10
Decision-Making Teams

E xtending the concept of team management down to the day-to-day operational level is a concept called Autonomous Small Work Groups (SWGs). Small work groups such as these provide greater autonomy and decentralization to operations personnel. They are essentially an evolution of participative practices like quality circles and JIT.

SWGs have allowed operational-level personnel to be mostly autonomous in the following types of activities:

- Production planning, scheduling, and dispatching
- Control of resources, inventory, and material handling
- Quality planning and process control
- Methods improvement
- Equipment setup, programming, operation, and maintenance
- Determining problems and coordinating corrective action[1]

One organization that has had a great deal of experience in this area is General Electric. In G.E.'s circuit-breaker business they were facing severe competition. To be competitive they had to reduce the delay in the time it took to solve problems and make decisions on the factory floor.

Their solution was to get rid of all line supervisors and quality inspectors, thereby reducing organizational layers between workers and the plant manager from three to one. Everything those middle managers used to handle (vacation scheduling, quality, work rules, and so forth) became the responsibility of the 129 workers on the factory floor. They were divided into teams of fifteen to twenty employees. What G.E. discovered was that the more responsibility they gave them, the faster problems were solved and decisions made.

Today, the plant basically runs itself. On the factory wall is a large electronic sign that informs employees how long it is taking them to make each circuit breaker box, how many boxes they have to make that day, and how many they have made so far. Employees pace themselves and make their own scheduling decisions. One worker emphasized, "I like to be my own boss. I don't like to be told what to do. I know if I can't get it done in eight hours, I can do it in ten without getting permission for overtime. We're behind right now. No one has to tell us we have to work Saturday."[2]

Characteristics of SWGs

SWGs are becoming a popular management tool. *Fortune* magazine even featured the concept of autonomous work groups, which they labeled "super teams," on the cover of a May 1990 issue. These essentially self-managed teams have drawn praise from a variety of quarters. Corning's CEO, Jamie Houghton, whose company has three thousand teams says, "If you really believe in quality, when you cut through everything, it's empowering your people, and it's empowering your people that leads to teams."[3]

SWGs have generally been used at step I and II of the Horizontal Management Continuum (see figure 6–1), but as we shall see in the next chapter, there is no reason why they could not be used for strategic decision making (step V). SWGs do the daily managerial activities usually reserved for operational supervisors in the traditional vertical organization. This includes managing such things as scheduling work, setting profit targets, hiring, and firing. Members may even know each other's salary.

SWGs usually consist of three to thirty workers and frequently mix blue-and white-collar workers. Sometimes they are a permanent part of the decision making—a structural figure. In other cases, they are created on an ad hoc basis. This situation might occur when one needs to put together a product-development team or to solve a very specific problem or to focus on a particular opportunity. SWGs are used in services as well as manufacturing. In "a recent survey of 476 Fortune 1,000 companies published by the American Productivity and Quality Center in Houston, while only 7 percent of the work force is organized in self-managed teams, half of those companies questioned say they will be relying significantly more on them in the years ahead."[4]

SWGs in Action

One company that has wide experience with SWGs is Hoechst Celanese Corporation. At the corporation's Celco plant in Narrows, Virginia, Sam McNair, the supervisor of a nine-person production group, says he likes to think of himself as a supervisor without subordinates. Their team is unusual in that everyone in the group is a decision maker and a generalist ready to play every position. As Jeanne Smith, Marketing Department specialist noted, "There are no sharp lines of authority."[5] Obviously, with a true SWG there are no supervisors and, in fact, at the plant the supervisor acts more as a coordinator.

What Hoechst Celanese gets out of their SWGs is both sounder decisions and better support since each member understands the rationale behind the decisions. The enthusiasm for such an arrangement can be contagious. When the first five jobs in the Celco group were posted, over one hundred of the plant's employees bid for them. They narrowed the number of candidates by reviewing past performance and by focusing on the characteristics they wanted from employees.

These characteristics included the need to be flexible, reliable, and have a strong ability to *learn*. The ability to learn was critical because each member of the team would have to be a generalist. If things went well, employee members would act as operators. If there were breakdowns, they could be repair persons. Likewise, when procedures were in doubt, they would be problem solvers, and when the product needed to be analyzed, they would be lab technicians.

When problems occur, such as an emergency repair, team members solve them on the spot. If decisions are more complicated, they can confer with each other. One of the team members, Ellis Martin, says you learn to trust the person who knows more about something than you do. Some members are better at one thing; others are better at others. Fred Thompson comments, "We'll ask each other and listen and learn. When you learn something hands-on, it's more enjoyable. You never get bored."[6]

Many companies have used SWGs to improve profits. Federal Express, for example, has made effective use of teams to improve productivity of its "back office" operations. They organized one thousand clerical employees into teams of five to ten, gave them the training and the authority to manage themselves. It helped the company improve service glitches like incorrect billing and lost packages by 13 percent in 1989.[7]

If significant savings can occur from simply getting operational personnel together and giving them more authority and responsibility, can you imagine what would happen if we could engage them in developing and implementing strategic decisions? Many are beginning to tap this enormous potential, realizing there is very little that operational personnel cannot understand or do. Examples of organizations making use of employees in strategic areas appropriate to steps III, IV, or V is still rare, but they exist and they are increasing in popularity.

Work Design Teams

So far we have focused on teams that were involved in running the daily operations, but teams are also being used to actually design work and work relationships. This is structural decision making at its most potent.

Hoechst Celanese Corporation is a highly diversified organization with a decentralized managerial philosophy and, as already noted, extensive experience with teams and team management. Their SWGs make decisions and solve problems in a variety of areas including those involving a department's organization and annual goals, product quality, and scheduling.

Depending on how they are used, these teams represent either step I, II, or III on the Horizontal Continuum identified in figure 6–1. Their step I teams are organized around a concept they call "ownership of machine." This essentially means the operator is responsible for everything about keeping machines running including starting up, shutting down, identifying malfunctions, and taking care of breakdowns.[8] Bill Batson, one of their supervisors, says that operators are running their own business, and that supervisors for these teams are more like coaches and resource people for the teams.

At Hoechst Celanese's Salisbury, North Carolina, fibers plant, their SWGs were used to improve the plant's effectiveness by making team members into managers. They can make the tough managerial decisions. When three members of a thirty-two-person team left, the remaining members decided not to replace them. In a more typical vertical organization, this type of decision would normally be made by supervisors rather than the workers. One of the operators in the group explained their logic, "Even though we were told we could replace them, we decided we could handle the work load by reassigning crew schedules."

Three years before this, the team had decided they could operate with seven fewer people, including one supervisor. This type of decision making is typical of step II on the Horizontal Continuum. It represents what used to be the daily managerial decision making reserved for lower and middle managers. This type of delegation is common at the two-thousand-employee Salisbury plant.

The corporation calls one particular type of team development approach "work design." In a task force style, teams representing particular work areas examine both internal and external factors affecting their jobs. These include safety, quality, productivity, customer-service, and employee-satisfaction concerns. Operators' specific decisions include determining "vacation and work scheduling, reviewing requests for appropriations, seeking peer performance input, and giving input on corrective action."[9]

When teams are doing a work-design project at the plant, they begin by evaluating the current work situation. As part of this process, employees on these work-design projects are given an overview of the business, which includes learning about import trends, cost pressures, and their product's market outlook.

Next, they look at how the technical aspects of their jobs can be improved, including how to improve communications and working relations. They focus on how to make their jobs more interesting. In anticipation of changing responsibilities, they also learn problem-solving and conflict-resolution techniques so they can better manage their new responsibilities. Their decision-making latitude is fairly broad. Once teams gather the information they need to make decisions, a plant steering committee usually accepts the team's proposals, only verifying that the choices fall within corporate boundaries (equal opportunity, length of service, equity, safety).

Organizational Design

One of the more impressive cases where employee teams were used to design a more effective work arrangement involved Hoechst Celanese Chemical Group's Clear Lake, Texas, plant. Here 129 craftspeople and first-line supervisors helped design a more effective organization.

In helping develop this new organizational structure, Ralph Schwausch, manager of Engineering and Maintenance, said they wanted to get everyone involved so everyone would have a sense of ownership and a stake in their success. The end result was an arrangement that gave greater responsibility to craftspeople. As a result, they are involved in planning routine jobs, screening job candidates, and deciding on the distribution of crafts within an area.

Creating this reorganization began by forming a team of all seven managers, the 129 craftspeople and first-line supervisors, as well as the 24 maintenance engineers and planners. Together, they developed a mission statement which read, "As part of the plant team, we maintain and improve plant facilities and provide quality services in a safe, efficient manner."[10] To design an organization that met this mission statement, management held meetings with craftspeople and agreed that a decentralized arrangement consisting of craftspeople and first-line supervisors in each unit would provide services quicker and more efficiently.

Before craftspeople had been in and out of an area, and no one took responsibility. Now, electricians, maintenance people, and others are in the same places every day and keep everything better maintained. In order to enhance services, they decided to change the way jobs were planned. Before, a unit would write a request for services (RFS) and send it to a maintenance supervisor who would send it to a planner, who sent it to a scheduler, who sent it to a craftsperson. "It took longer to do that than it did to do the job," notes Annette Kyle, section leader of Instruments and Electrical.[11]

Now supervisors bypass the RFS system by writing out small jobs without involving their planners and schedulers by simply placing a request in a box outside their office. Craftspeople pick them up as soon as they are free. Backlogs have been cut in half, and red tape has been cut dramatically. People feel empowered. When delegation is designed in from the beginning, exciting things happen. In this case, employees worked better when those who did the work designed how the work was to be organized.

Strategic Input

One case where employees were brought into strategic decision making was at Johnsonville Foods in Sheboygan, Wisconsin. There employees helped CEO Ralph Stayer make a decision to proceed with a major plant expansion.[12] Ralph Stayer was contacted by a major food company and asked to manufacture sausage under a private label. The additional work would have overloaded the plant and forced employees to work very long hours. Before he declined the offer, he assembled his employees, told them the situation, then asked them if they wanted the business and what they wanted to do.

Employees at Johnsonville are organized into teams of five to twenty employees. They were told the good side, which was essentially that they would make more money (because of bonuses associated with the company's profitability). They were told the bad news; namely, it meant long hours, strained machinery, and the risk of declining quality.

The teams at Johnsonville deliberated ten days before they told Stayer their answer. They told him they could and wanted to do it by working seven days a week at first so their work would level off later. They decided how much new machinery and new people that would need. They decided how much work per day they would need to meet the schedule. The end result was that the job was taken and productivity has risen by 50 percent.[13]

The efforts at Johnsonville represent an effort to incorporate employee teams into step V horizontal decision making. Strategic decision-making teams do not even have to be limited to project decisions like Johnsonville's.

Steering Teams

Texas Instrument's (TI) vice-president of their semiconductor group, James Watson, notes that control and direction can still exist when one uses a team approach.[14] They do not have to be limited strictly to the operational day-to-day level decisions. Teams can be used throughout the organization.

In TI's chip factory in Texas, James Watson created a hybrid team approach using a hierarchy (vertical) of teams (horizontal). On the top was a *steering team* consisting of the plant manager and department heads of manufacturing, finance, engineering, and human resources. This team set strategy and had the final approval of large projects. Their most important responsibility was to show interest in the team below them.

Directly under this team were three teams: the *corrective action team,* the *quality-improvement team,* and the *effective team.* The first two teams were cross-functional and consisted mainly of middle managers and professionals like engineers and accountants. The effectiveness teams consisted entirely of blue-collar employees.

Corrective action teams are special project teams that handle short-term problems, then disband. In contrast, the quality improvement teams work on long-term projects such as streamlining the manufacturing process. When asked how he helped the teams from becoming just another hierarchy, Watson said he kept changing the teams and tried to remain responsive to changing business conditions.

Business Sense

Team members must understand the entire business operation to assume some responsibility for strategic and financial decisions (step IV and V on the Horizontal Continuum). That is a lesson Chaparral Steel understands well. Chaparral Steel has long been noted for its use of teams to improve performance.

Team workers at Chaparral Steel are effective because they are trained to understand the whole business operation. They learn to improve their decision-making skills by going through a series of courses the company calls the Chaparral Process. In these courses employees not only understand how steel moves through the company, but also learn finance, accounting, and sales. Employees understand how they fit in and how they relate to the entire organization. Financial statements are posted monthly in the mill, including a chart tracking profits before taxes—the key measure for profit sharing.[15]

An example of Chaparral Steel's approach toward team building occurred in the early 1980s. The company created a team with one team leader and three millworkers. They were evaluating expensive equipment used to flatten and shape steel. As part of this process, this special project team made several trips to inspect equipment in South America, Europe, and Asia. They selected the equipment they felt was best. The team then ordered it from Germany, oversaw its installation, and even negotiated the contracts for the work that was required.[16] It is the type of comprehensive decision making that is possible with team management when members have the authority and knowledge needed.

Self-regulating System

Teams working on special projects as above or on product development, as mentioned earlier, can be a potent tool for competitiveness. One company that carried the use of team management further than most is a specialty chemical plant located in LaPorte, Texas. *All* sixty-seven employees at the plant are active in management decision making and frequently do a variety of tasks without supervision. Employees on these teams have the power to evaluate their coworkers' performance, discipline those employees whose behavior they consider unacceptable, and even hire new employees.[17]

The plant, Rohm and Haas Bayport Inc., is run by plant manager Robert D. Gilbert. He believes too much hierarchy keeps companies from being productive. When asked about why he had made the change, he said he had "wanted to create a workplace where people could be responsible and at the same time be involved in managing their own work."[18]

The original plant was very much a vertical organization. Gilbert reduced their levels from four to three. Gilbert was at the top of the organization. Directly reporting to him were the financial analysts, the personnel manager, and the manufacturing managers of the plant's two operations. The third and last level consists of administrative teams of office technicians who report to the financial analyst and the personnel manager. The other functional teams on this level report to their respective manufacturing managers.

The concept that this organization is a three-level, vertical organization may be a misnomer since the functional teams and administrative team are connected to each other by the management team (Gilbert and the four positions reporting to him). It would seem to resemble more of a network arrangement rather than rigid levels. Special project teams are formed as needed to solve ad hoc problems that occur.

In order for self-regulating teams to work, team members must be knowledgeable in a wide variety of tasks. At Rohm and Haas Bayport, technicians do a variety of tasks, including working in the lab, working in material-handling areas, or other areas where they are needed. They rotate jobs with other teams, and employees are encouraged to learn all they can.

Employees within these teams are paid for acquiring new skills. Gilbert notes there are no job levels for their plant technicians. Instead, it is a pay-for-skills system. He also says they do not give merit since measuring and evaluating job performance of two people on a team did not encourage teamwork.[19]

An important part of the pay-for-skills system is their performance evaluation system for technicians. Originally, technicians in each operation completed a written evaluation on each other every six months and then gave them to the manufacturing manager of their operation. The results of the evaluation were then reviewed and discussed one-on-one with the person being evaluated.

Over time the evaluation process changed so that technicians actually began evaluating each other at face-to-face meetings. Technicians now only rate members of teams and the teams that relieve them. Their evaluation is based on several areas, including safety, self-regulation, teamwork, production, unit operations, and other factors. Each individual was rated from one (unsatisfactory) to five (satisfactory).

At first one might think that such a system would be very popular with employees. Their Bayport plant experienced a 50 percent turnover rate during its first two years of operation. Since that time the selection process has improved and the turnover is less than five percent. Gilbert points out that they improved their selection process after they had experience working with people in the plant.[20] Adapting to "short ladders" and organizations that are becoming increasingly horizontal can be as difficult for some employees as it is for some managers.

Concluding Thoughts

Teams are becoming a vital part of the emergence of the new horizontal organization. As management begins to concentrate on empowering the organization, organizational teams will be essential. Many organizations, such as Globe and others, are deeply involved with using network teams to enhance their quality, productivity, or reduce costs.

Many more organizations have gone beyond communication and co-ordination networks toward actually changing the structure of the organizational lines of authority and decision making. Often these new relationships have begun with the introduction of product development. *Concurrent engineering* attempts to make "seamless" the separate areas of process design and product development.

Team management has gone far beyond joint or collaborative decision making in product and process arrangements. It is being used throughout the entire organizational structure. Autonomous work groups, like those at G.E., are being used extensively at the operational level.

This team arrangement can be of enormous benefit to those supervisors who remain. With Hoechst Celanese Corporation's new system of teams, the supervisor's role has changed. One of their supervisors, Walter Forbes, notes that he can now spend 40 percent of his time away from the factory floor. Instead of being on the floor, he now has more time to get involved in long-range projects and serve on his own teams, such as the company's quality improvement team. He spends much of the remaining time coaching employees on teamwork.

Today, these lower-level operational teams are gradually evolving to the point where they are increasingly used for higher-level design, financial, and even strategic concerns. As we have seen in this chapter, given enough experience, training, and trust in self-management, these teams have begun to evolve into a kind of self-regulating system.

144 • *Beyond Customer Satisfaction*

Notes

1. Michael Wall, "Quality Assurance in Participative Organizations," *1990 International Industrial Engineering Conference Proceedings*, San Francisco, California, May 1990, p. 444.
2. Brian Dumaine, "How Managers Can Succeed through Speed" *Fortune*, February 13, 1989, p. 56.
3. Brian Dumaine, "Who Needs A Boss?" *Fortune*, 7 May, 1990, p. 52.
4. Ibid., p. 52.
5. Frances O. Connell, "Who's On Second? Everyone," *Reporter* 4, no. 1 (Winter 1990), p. 8.
6. Ibid., p. 9.
7. Dumaine, p. 54.
8. Kay Bender Braun, "A Tale of Two Teams," *Reporter* 5, no. 1 (Spring 1990), p. 19.
9. Stme, Andrea, "Design for Decision Making" *Reporter,* Vol. 3, no. 2, July, 1989, p. 8.
10. Susan Ainsworth, "160 Heads Are Better Than 1," *Reporter* 3, no. 3 (Fall 1989), p. 17.
11. Ibid., p. 17.
12. Dumaine, p. 53.
13. Ibid., p. 53.
14. Ibid., p. 55.
15. Dumaine, p. 58.
16. Ibid., p. 58.
17. William H. Wagel, "Working (and Managing) Without Supervisors," *Personnel* 64, no. 9 (September 1987), p. 8.
18. Ibid., p. 8.
19. Ibid., p. 8.
20. Ibid., p. 8.

11

Restructuring at the Macro Level

I n the past chapter we looked at how companies were implementing a more horizontal approach at the lowest level of the organization. Some of the companies are even experimenting with middle-or higher-level delegation of authority and decision making. One question, naturally, comes to mind. Is there a limit to how far this decentralization can go? I think not.

Even at the most macro level we are starting to see greater decentralization. Corporations are doing more restructuring of their subsidiaries and divisions within worldwide organizations, trying to create an entrepreneurial spirit. Enormous strides are being made in decentralizing, even at the highest level. With this freedom comes certain risk. How does a corporation control these divisions and subsidiaries while still encouraging freedom and initiative? What is to prevent anarchy? How can management philosophy and practices be transferred within a decentralized corporation? Two highly successful corporations, Glaxo Holding, Inc., and General Electric, show how to control and transfer management practices at these levels.

Glaxo is probably the lesser known of the two among U.S. managers. While Glaxo may not be well known, it is no small operation. Glaxo is a $4 billion pharmaceutical company headquartered in the United Kingdom. It is one of the world's best-performing companies. They have virtually come from nowhere in the 1960s to being the number-three drug company in the world, as well as one of the world's fastest growing pharmaceutical companies in the 1990s.

In 1977 they had $200 million in sales. By 1988, it was $1 billion, and in 1989 it was $1.6 billion. They have tripled their market share in five years and have had a 40 percent growth rate over a twenty-five-year period. Their great success is largely due to having good products (like Zantac, the ulcer-fighting drug), and most importantly from a management perspective, a philosophy that uses decentralization as a major strategic weapon.

Jawahar S. Sawardeker, vice-president of Technical Affairs for Glaxo (Latin America), Inc., said several factors have led to their growth.[1] One is the ability of their management to focus the corporation. He made the point that unless you know where you are headed, you are in trouble. That means having a sharp definition of the business you are in and the kind of business you want to be in.

Glaxo is in the discovery, development, manufacturing, and marketing of prescription products. They are focused in one direction. At one time they received a lot of their revenue from agricultural products, food supplements, vitamins, and even the hospital furniture business. Certainly this is not a universal prescription for management success (many successful companies are very diversified), but it works for Glaxo. They chose to focus exclusively on pharmaceuticals, and it has provided the central plan for their organization.

Glaxo's Philosophy

Sawardeker notes that Glaxo Holding, the parent company, intends to compete in every country. They do this because they take the long-term view of their business. Their focus is not the next quarterly earning report. Anyone can do that, Sawardeker said. It is not even the next six months; they remain fixed on the long term. Glaxo intends to be a market leader, and to do so they have to stay strategically located in every country where they market their products.

To this end, they have made a commitment to quality, since it is the quality of your product and services by which the world judges you. In the world marketplace it has been said that you do not have to worry about those companies that do not care about quality because they will not be in business very long.

Glaxo insures quality in their products by a process of *validation* that involves collecting and documenting evidence that over time a manufacturing process will deliver the product within the predetermined specifications. Glaxo does this validating with everything. No process is acceptable unless it is validated. No procedure is acceptable unless it is validated. No computer program is acceptable unless it is validated.

The company sets great stock in the value of standards, so it is essential that every procedure is validated. Measurement and standards are vital parts of their day-to-day operation. They not only measure their quality, they make complete use of the data by doing trend analysis to look for overall patterns. This is a practice different from that of most companies, who will measure something and if it meets specs, they put the paper and data away. Sawardeker said Glaxo spends an enormous amount of time evaluating and studying this data and using techniques like trend analysis to maximize the potential of the data.

Like most organizations, Glaxo's lifeblood is the flow of information throughout the company. They know they can enhance their competitiveness if they improve the transfer of information. They do this by creating a *network of autonomous national units*. Their philosophy might be defined as "Think globally—Act locally." They give each of their subsidiaries the product, capital, and, most importantly, the authority to build their own business as they see fit. Sawardeker believes it is this freedom that makes the difference. This freedom allows the spirit of entrepreneurism to exist throughout their subsidiaries.

Hire the best people, believe in them, give them the power, and leave them alone. That may be their philosophy, but this does not mean abdication of leadership. It does not mean lack of control. It does not mean anarchy. The parent company, Glaxo Holding, sets the policy as to how business should be conducted, but it is up to the local company to determine how to implement it.

Their approach is similar to a venture capitalist. Local managers look up to general managers for resources and capital and then measure their performance based on profit and loss. For instance, when Glaxo Holding set up their American operation, the American subsidiary built it exactly as they pleased. It was built with local people, local talent, and no approval was needed from the parent company.

Transferring Leadership

Any successful company must have leadership. The vice-president of their Latin American division emphasized that Glaxo does not wait for leaders to come along. They seek potential leaders, recognize them, and try to develop leaders at all levels. Glaxo continuously tries to get all their management people together and keep them informed. They talk about capital, ventures, inventory, sales, or how the business is doing. They try to make a point of simply walking up and sharing all types of information.

Leadership flourishes because of the culture. Glaxo is one company where innovation is encouraged and that has a culture that accepts reasonable risks. Valuing changes means that one must accept the risk that failure will occur. For subordinates to learn, regardless of their position, their managers must allow them to take reasonable risks.

The other side of freedom is accountability. The purpose of this accountability is not so much to point a finger as it is to provide guidance for individuals or for whole subsidiaries. It would seem that Glaxo Holding sees itself as a good parent who encourages independence and experimentation of their subsidiaries, while preventing fatal mistakes. For freedom and autonomy to be possible and encouraged, there must be constraints, according to Sawardeker. As noted earlier, his company emphasizes quality. To that end, there can be no autonomy. No group can ignore the quality imperative. Every entity within Glaxo has quality standards.

For Glaxo, even in the manufacturing process there can be no autonomy. Subsidiaries must conform to the manufacturing process the parent company has specified. If someone wants to change it, they have to go to their center, get approval, and provide supporting data. There are obviously constraints on the financial side that require approval. Sawardeker did indicate that each has fairly large approval authorities. His boss can allocate up to £1 million without additional approval.

Rules and standards need not be restraining, but they are needed for conducting business. When making a major capital expenditure, like building a new facility, the decision must go through Glaxo's technical committee, which looks at standards and debates the facility's impact on those standards. The debate usually centers on whether or not decisions are within technical standards. It is managerial freedom, but it is freedom with constraints built into the decision.

Glaxo emphasizes setting standards and developing standardized processes and procedures as a means of delegating authority and decision making. Obviously, it is possible that such a reliance on standards and standardization of process and procedures could create a bureaucratic rigidity and destroy the very freedom and entrepreneurial spirit they are trying to create. Such a risk is always possible when basing management decisions on whether certain standards are met or not.

Although Glaxo uses standardized operating procedures, they say they are flexible in that standards can be changed overnight. If someone does have a valid change, all they must do is go through a review procedure so they do not accidentally change something on line that is not supposed to be changed. Standards do not have to create rigidity as they truly can be changed and there are simple procedures to change them. It is absolutely essential that such a system is in place; otherwise, it is mostly bureaucracy that is created rather than entrepreneurism.

Transferring Management Practice

Previously we discussed the need to transfer leadership, but leadership is not the only thing that needs to be transferred. Glaxo's use of standards is one way of transferring managerial practices. It also provides a means of decentralizing leadership. If standards and policies are clear, it is easier to delegate, to decentralize.

One company that has made great strides in transferring managerial practices throughout their corporation is General Electric (G.E.). As you may recall from the previous chapter, G.E. is a highly diversified corporation with thirteen divisions. It is a huge $55 billion revenue corporation that allows wide autonomy among its divisions. Despite the diverse nature of G.E.'s divisions and the need for greater speed and flexibility through greater decision-making autonomy within each division, there is still a need for coordination. Each division must reflect the G.E. perspective and direction; otherwise, anarchy might exist with each operating its own fiefdom.

John Welch, CEO for G.E., talks about "integrated diversity" when explaining their approach. Specifically, the idea of integrated diversity is to try to get their thirteen separate divisions helping each other rather than operating as so many "loose cannons." Welch emphasized that most diversified companies are able to transfer technical resources and dollars across their business. Others do a good job transferring human resources. He says G.E. does "the best job of transferring management practices across our business—the best techniques, the best systems ideas, the best generic management principles that will produce consistently rapid growth and superior profitability."[2]

To achieve this they begin by dismantling layer after layer of management. At one time they had nine layers of management. They have reduced to four layers in some cases. They also changed the corporate headquarter's traditional role. "The role of the staff was turned 180 degrees from checker, inquisitor, and authority figure to facilitator, helper, and supporter of 'the field'—our thirteen businesses."[3]

Today all thirteen divisions report to Welch and his vice-chairmen, Lawrence A. Bossidy and Edward E. Hood. While the businesses are very diverse—from television networks to financial services to plastic—each shares management practices that help bind them together and create their integrated diversity. This occurs despite the fact that each division is run with little daily interference from headquarters.

One of the division leaders, John D. Opie, head of G.E. Lighting, says when someone asks why he does not quit and run his own company, he responds that he is "already running a billion dollar business."[4] Welch does seem to provide his leaders with freedom. Rather than evaluating their decisions in great detail, he often takes no more than an afternoon to review some strategic plans or major capital expansion program. Welch and his top officials keep in touch with division heads mainly by telephone.

Cross-fertilization

A cross-fertilization analogy could be used to explain how G.E. transfers management throughout their corporation. It can be thought of as cross-training at the very highest levels. Cross-fertilization begins at their Management Development Institute in Crotonville, New York, where five thousand employees a year share what they have learned in areas like customer service, product development, or other generic subjects. Then every January, G.E. gathers their top five hundred managers for two-and-a-half days in Boca Raton, Florida.[5] These five hundred come from all of their diversified businesses.

Cross-fertilization actually begins at these meetings long before the formal presentation by participants. It is done informally with marketing managers from the various business divisions seeking each other out for advice and suggestions.

Later in the year (October), an even more select group of one hundred G.E. managers attend another two-and-a-half day get-together. The sharing here is of a more strategic and generic nature, concerning topics such as acquisitions, mergers, and expansions. Finally, transferring of management practice occurs through quarterly meetings of their Corporate Executive Council (CEC). These meetings involve thirty to forty senior G.E. executives along with Welch and his two vice-chairmen. Topics are very broad in nature, including subjects like economic conditions, capital spending programs, and more specific ones like pay plans, drug testing, and stock options.

At these meetings each of G.E.'s businesses can propose their own plan or program. The proposal then goes through a screening process, much like the approach used by Glaxo Holding, to make sure it makes good sense. In these meetings they do not approve details, but they do want to know the details so they can see which programs are working. When something does work, they can let their other areas know of their successes.

G.E. helps integrate leadership by posing specific questions that help get everyone on the same wavelength. For instance, in their 1986 meeting of the top one hundred executives they asked each of the leaders of their thirteen businesses to present a one-page answer to five questions. These were: "What are your market dynamics globally today, and where are they going over the next several years?" "What actions have your competitors taken in the last three years to upset those global dynamics?" "What have you done in the last three years to accept those dynamics?" "What are the most dangerous things your competitors could do in the next three years to upset those dynamics?" "What are the most effective things you could do to bring your desired impact on those dynamics?"[6]

G.E. believes that as they eliminate bureaucracy and create a more integrated organization, it is essential to share the best practices of each area, ask questions about those practices, and use simple listening. Their goal is to create a "boundary-less" company by eliminating walls that separate departments and companies. In creating their own form of horizontal management, they are trying to eliminate barriers between engineering, marketing, sales, and customer service. They want no distinctions between domestic and foreign operations. The objective is to ignore labels. They believe that labels like "management, salaried, or hourly" get in the way of work.

Concluding Thoughts

Horizontal management in many ways is a grassroots movement. The most common application of horizontal management has been at the lowest operational level and the most popular technique has been the use of team management. Line-of-site teams and multidiscipline teams are being used to replace first-level and even second-level managers. Horizontal management has also been occurring sporadically at higher levels. There are product-development teams and teams to implement special policies and programs. The current emphasis on quality and customer-satisfaction teams is one example.

Horizontal management at the highest step, the strategic and policy realm, is much rarer. G.E. and Glaxo are two companies where decentralization is occurring at the highest, multinational, multidivisional level. In their own ways, each is trying to decentralize and redefine the mission of corporate headquarters. Rather than acting as an inquisitor, a controller, they are trying to use corporate headquarters as an integrator, a helper, or a coach. It is much too soon to see if it is working but at least they are trying.

Horizontal management at the highest level means creating a network of autonomous national units as in Glaxo's case, or semiautonomous divisions as in G.E.'s case. Corporate headquarters may set policies, but their style is more venture capitalist. They provide the resources, the "seed" money, but stay out of the daily activities. Performance is measured by profit and loss, not on detailed, day-to-day accounting.

The trick is to avoid both anarchy and excessive control. Decentralization must be validated to be practical. There needs to be a process to insure that the various divisions or national units are meeting predetermined specifications. Glaxo calls this process "validation," and they do it by making extensive use of workplace data, trend analysis, and other statistical evaluators.

G.E. also has a system of standards that must be met by its subdivisions before approval is granted. However, both Glaxo and G.E. insure flexibility by allowing these divisions to have a great deal of autonomy at the divisional and national levels.

This is managerial freedom, but freedom with constraints. Of course, there is always the risk that these constraints will destroy the freedom they are trying to protect. For that reason, it is important to remember that if standards are to be used, they must also be frequently reviewed and changed if needed. Unless it is easy to change standards, there is a real risk of creating bureaucracy rather than entrepreneurism.

Having a measure of flexible control creates a system where corporate-wide decentralization can occur, but there must be more. Truly dynamic organizations are more than a system; they have a unique personality. Leadership at the corporate level must be transferred to each unit for each of those units to feel like they are on the same team. Each individual national unit or division must reflect something of the personality of the team.

For the whole to be greater than the individual parts, leadership must be transferred. G.E.'s ability to transfer this leadership and management practices within a decentralized philosophy appears as good as anyone's. They do it simply and effectively. There is open sharing of information and cross-fertilization. The diverse members hold frequent meetings. Bonding occurs when each shares what they have learned and each is focused on concerns that affect the corporation as a whole.

Notes

1. Comments made at the *International Conference on Industrial Engineering*, San Francisco, California, 20–23 May 1990.
2. Stephen W. Quickel, "Welch on Welch," *Financial World* 159, no. 7 (3 April 1990), p. 62.
3. *1989 Annual Report*, General Electric, 1989, p. 4.
4. Quickel, p. 4.
5. Ibid., p. 4.
6. Noel Tichy and Ram Charan, "Speed, Simplicity, Self-Confidence," *Harvard Business Review*, September–October 1989, p. 115.

Part IV
Creating a Compeer Culture

12
Compeer Culture

E arlier I mentioned the possibility of someday creating true equality within corporate organizations. Instead of "employees" and "bosses," one day we might see the emergence of "compeers." In the last four chapters we saw the emergence of techniques such as streamlining and team management that I believe make compeers more likely. Certainly, it is impossible to predict whether full equality will become a reality or not, but there is no doubt about the urgency of the need for preparing operational personnel to become fuller partners. Without the full support of these people, there is little chance that organizations can maintain the level of competitiveness and responsiveness essential to success in today's market.

Preparation of our *entire* work force begins with more effective training efforts. The greatest speeches by CEOs, the most innovative rewards, the most sincere efforts by management will mean nothing unless operational personnel are prepared to assume greater responsibility and authority.

Almost everyone recognizes the need for a work force better trained and better prepared to meet the challenges of the twenty-first century. However, few give the concept more than lip service. A recent survey of industrial engineers pointed out both the need for better educational preparation of the work force and, unfortunately, the lack of managerial attention it has received.[1]

Lack of educational preparation of our work force is the single greatest economic weakness of the United States, according to 33.5 percent of surveyed industrial engineers. It was ranked significantly higher than other topics that have received far greater publicity such as the the much-publicized need to improve our manufacturing base.

The need to improve our educational system was chosen far more often than other areas such as concern for quality, marketing, service, research, and even technology considerations. It was not just the educational system that was criticized. About 74 percent of those same engineers said less educated and poorly trained workers were hindering U.S. productivity.

The percentage was even higher when they were asked what was hindering the government's efficiency.

At least they know who to blame. Almost 80 percent of these engineers either strongly agree or somewhat agree with the statement that management lacks the commitment to implement productivity improvement programs, such as gain sharing and training programs for employees.

Training and Success

Contrast this lack of support to those companies who are highly committed to education and training. It is not a coincidence that these companies are extremely competitive. One example of a corporation committed to training and education is Motorola. On the average, Motorola provides their 102,000 employees with one million hours of training per year. In 1987 they spent $44 million on training. That represented 2.4 percent of their total corporate payroll.[2]

Motorola's training is extensive, especially in the area of quality. Forty percent of it is focused on quality. Perhaps, that is why they were the U.S.'s first winner of the Malcolm Baldridge quality award. It is doubtful that it was a coincidence since in just three years they created over 150 hours of quality-related training for their assembly operators, technicians, engineers, and support groups. These are the type of people that organizations desperately need to bring into the decision-making process. What better way to do it than by focusing the attention of these operations people on quality to give them a total organizational perspective?

Another important point of their educational process is its flexibility for the individual. Motorola makes use of "course managers" who help employees and their managers select programs to meet an individual's needs and the needs of the corporation. Motorola's educational process is not to be admired just because of its size and its extensiveness; rather, it is their rational, logical approach that is most impressive.

They bring all aspects of business into their efforts. They look at all areas, including products, service, manufacturing, non-manufacturing administration, and operations. The Motorola Training and Education Center (MTEC) is a university-style educational operation. MTEC provides product/process training, as well as other specific management training. In short, the emphasis is on providing *all* employees with the knowledge and skills necessary. Through their Management Institute (MMI), Motorola also has intensive two-week programs for senior and support level personnel, which focus on the development of decision-making skills.

Talk is cheap and, unfortunately, talking is one of the things upper management does all too well. Commitment is won through deeds and actions, not talk. Motorola and a few others have proven their commitment to enhancing their work force.

Cross-training

Cross-training is one of the most potent ways of developing people and implementing horizontal management at the operational level. It is also an extremely flexible tool that can enhance operational and strategic decision making. First we will look at the impact of cross-training at the operational level.

All vertical organizations consist of layers upon layers of highly specialized jobs. Vertical organizations are crippled by proliferation of a jungle of organizational titles and job classifications. The antithesis of this, and one advocated by proponents of horizontal management, would be for everyone to be a manager. If ever an organization reaches this point, it will truly be egalitarian. For now though there are far too many divisions, too many job classifications, and too many job restrictions.

This is quite obvious at the operational level in union shops where the myriad of job classifications severely limits what each worker can and cannot do. In a union shop, a foreman cannot do any production work, even in a crisis. Electricians have to call carpenters to straighten a crooked stud if they are installing a fuse box. A truck driver cannot load or unload his own truck! Employees cannot move from one job classification to another, but rather must do the same narrow job over and over. The center of attention is the list of work rules and restrictive job classifications, not what it takes to be effective.

There can be enormous saving, even at the lowest level, if cross-training is introduced. An article by Peter Drucker in the *Wall Street Journal* made the point that a contractor ran a study on one nonunion and one union crew doing identical projects. He found that the nonunion employees worked an average of fifty minutes out of every hour while the union crew worked only thirty-five and spent the remainder of the time waiting for someone to come back from the restroom or waiting for a journeyman to do jobs that an apprentice could have done.[3] The union crew required eight members; the nonunion crew only required five. It should be obvious by now why automakers have been insisting on reducing the number of job classifications in their work force.

Since more people can do more jobs, it is easier to manage an operation. For instance, if there are fewer job classifications, then it is easier to schedule work because it is easier to calculate the number of employees that will be needed. Likewise, as Drucker noted, more work gets done because one person is not waiting on another. In general, it increases the company's speed and flexibility while lowering overhead.

The Honda facility in Marysville, Ohio, and the Toyota facility in Fremont, California, function with only three to five job classifications. General Motors, Ford, and Chrysler each have about sixty. At G.E.'s lighting plant in Newark, Ohio, there are only four job categories compared to twenty-one at other G.E. lighting plants.[4]

Another example of cross-training at the operational level is the work team discussed in the previous chapter. Step II work teams do anything once done by a supervisor. Many call this use of teams "line of sight" management, because anything a team can see is the team's responsibility.

Managerial Cross-training

Cross-training should not be limited to blue-collar or other first-line operational jobs. All levels of management can benefit from cross-training. One company that uses managerial cross-training is the Pepsi-Cola Bottlers, Inc., facility located in Springfield, Missouri. Pepsi U.S.A. evaluates each bottler's quality by taking samples of their product at the production facility and at various stores where it is sold. Those bottlers with the highest quality receive an award called the Caleb Bradham Award. For ten years the Springfield bottler has received the award. They are also the only bottler to receive a 100 percent rating from Pepsi U.S.A. This means when the samples were taken at their production facility and the stores, absolutely no deviations from the standard were found.[5]

There are many reasons why the facility has been successful. There is a great deal of pride within the organization. They do all the standard testing done by all Pepsi bottlers, only they do this testing more frequently. Most bottlers test every hour, but they test their product every 15 minutes! When problems occur, production is halted until management is satisfied the problem has been corrected.

Each key manager started his or her career at the bottom, either as a route salesperson or on the production line. Of critical importance is not only understanding the whole business from the ground up, but understanding each other's part in the whole production process. All managers have *multiple responsibilities*. Each manager knows what is involved in the other managers' jobs. This is not simply the normal cursory knowledge among departments; instead, this is intimate knowledge. There are the normal production, marketing, sales, and finance managers as there are in any company, but each has several responsibilities in each area. Both the marketing manager and the production manager emphasize that, if needed, each could step in and run the other's department. They said that also applies to all other managers and all other areas of the organization at that plant.

Deep and Broad Expertise

A manager told me that once experts had been the fashion. These experts were just that—experts in a narrow area of specialization, but they were usually incapable of understanding areas outside their tightly focused specialties. It was not easy for these people to form interdisciplinary teams because they had great difficulty communicating with others.

Then came the day of the well-rounded manager who had a lot of breadth, but not much depth. These people communicated reasonably well and understood many things reasonably well, but never quite well enough.

The challenges facing modern business can only be met by a person who has both depth and breadth. Such a person starts out with something he or she knows well and learns the adjacent disciplines also. Pepsi's managers at the Springfield plant are such people. I have no doubt that compeers in a totally flat, totally horizontal organization will be the same.

Pepsi's approach is not the only way to bring about broad and deep expertise. Another way might be through giving operational personnel all the financial information they need to be as well informed as any manager. That is the approach taken by Springfield Remanufacturing Company (SRC). SRC has been extremely successful. They have been featured in *INC* magazine and in the PBS special "Growing A Business." One of their managers noted, "We have experienced almost a 300 percent growth in business, but only a 20 percent increase in overhead costs." Everyone should take notice.[6]

SRC gets an enormous amount of energy and ability out of their operational personnel. Their management approach has led to much of their success. The trust, openness, and delegation at SRC is simply decades beyond ordinary American management practice. As Jack Stack, president of SRC, is fond of saying, "There is not a (financial) number our employees don't know about or don't have access to."[7]

He believes that managers usually fail to reach their employees true level of intelligence. He further believes that if all employees knew what he and his other top managers knew, they would make essentially the same decisions he does. To that end, he keeps everyone top to bottom (especially bottom) intimately informed of the company's financial vital statistics. He teaches them about income statements, balance sheets, and profits.

I myself have both taught college students and worked with blue-collar employees. It is my opinion that Jack Stack is absolutely correct, that even assembly-line employees know more about what is financially involved in running a company and what it takes to make one financially successful than the typical college graduate. Stack calls it teaching the worker the "great game of business."

They use several nontraditional but effective learning tools. Their program is grounded in the fact that the company itself is employee-owned and operated, so each worker is already a part owner. This fact alone does not explain their success. Many ESOPs have failed, and most never create the trust nor support from operational people that SRC has achieved.

They have bonus programs which can mean as much as a ten percent increase in a person's income. These bonus programs are well managed with each bonus being tied directly into the financial health of the company and each person's department. Still, that alone is not enough. The difference at SRC is that every employee has complete access to all financial information pertinent to the company's operations. Every employee knows what financial effect his or her actions have on the success of SRC as a whole.

Overhead Budgets

In the past, first-line supervisors and other operational and staff personnel have been nurtured to develop more depth to grow through something they call a commodity or overhead budget. In most businesses, as with SRC, someone is in charge of controlling expenses in a particular area or department. This is typical, but SRC believes relying on this alone leads to dishonesty and ineffectiveness for it is common practice for managers to do everything possible to spend the money allocated to their departments by the end of the year so they can be assured the same amount for the next fiscal year.

SRC avoids many of these problems by its practice of extremely open and frank discussion on a weekly basis about all the financial aspects of the business. As many managers give back money or reduce their own budget as those who request additional money. Remember, all are part owners, and they behave accordingly. Although their shares may not be that significant, they treat them as if they were.

SRC has encouraged financial responsibility, team play, and cooperation through the use of overhead budgets. This involves requesting volunteer supervisors and managers throughout the company to monitor the use of particular commodities (e.g. chemicals, abrasives, packaging, etc.) plant-wide. Controlling all expenditures of these commodities means these volunteer supervisors and managers must control everything from copy-machine fluid to industrial cleaners. It is great management cross-training since the participants get to see the entire organization.

Mike Carrigan, vice-president of SRC, says he uses it as a teaching tool so young managers learn the importance of budgets and avoid dishonesty. Since they are the one in charge of the entire commodity, there is no stealing or padding. There is nothing to gain.

Reducing the Distance

Financial disclosure may not reduce the number of vertically organized levels in a company, but it improves performance because it reduces the distance between levels. There is less likelihood of communication or motivational problems when each employee understands the "big picture." SRC's approach works because there is a corporate policy of open communication about the budgetary process. Profits, losses, and even investment decisions are there for all to see. There is an air of trust built on openness and respect down to the lowest level. There is no "need to know" restriction here; Stack feels everyone needs to know if they are going to be as excited about the business as he is.

The Pepsi General Bottler's use of multi-responsibility is a very traditional yet effective means of reducing the distance between levels. It may even be one of the ways of eliminating the levels. After all, if everyone does the same thing and understands all of what is going on, why have divisions and levels? SRC uses the budget and financial disclosure and detailed financial responsibilities at even its lowest levels as a means of training and educating its people.

Undoubtedly, implementing financial openness as SRC has done is essential to developing the type of employee we will need in the twenty-first century. Having employees who know the who, what, where, when, and, most importantly, the why of running a company is essential. SRC is already there; others will have to follow as the need grows more urgent to have our employees who can handle greater responsibility and authority.

Joint Management

Despite SRC's innovation, most of the final decisions for how and what training employees and others receive remains in the hands of upper management. How much more energy within an organization would exist if *all* personnel within the organization jointly decided the hows and whys? Perhaps that is the kind of training that may be common in the next century. Sound ridiculous? There is already a very traditional, highly vertical organization that in the early 1980s developed a unique joint-management approach that could be the prototype for companies of the future.

Ford Motor Company fashioned a system training and personal growth that seeks to satisfy both corporate and individual needs. Ford and their union, the UAW, have jointly created an effective training program that emphasized changing their corporate culture. Their educational and developmental activities are successful because they take a systems approach that is built on voluntary choices and a voluntary agenda. They are able to encourage innovation through codetermination and coresponsibility.

Employee Commitment

Paul Banas, manager of Employee Development and Planning at Ford, notes that "Employee commitment . . . is the bedrock of all corporate strategies" and that corporate "plans for the future will succeed or fail depending on how well the total employee team responds to them."[8] The real key to whether organizations will be successful in the future will depend on whether managers can learn how to nurture this employee commitment. In earlier chapters, we underscored the importance of obtaining commitment through employee involvement. There is another means of securing employee commitment.

Paul Banas of Ford stresses that "there also is great value in providing employees with meaningful opportunities for professional and personal development. It is the natural complement to employee cooperation and commitment. The more sophisticated, the more knowledgeable, and the more capable the members of the team are, the more they can contribute. A better educated and developed work force is vital not only to an employee's future, but is critical for our nation as well. Lifelong learning will be a requirement for every employee."[9]

A considerable amount of Ford's success rests on the fact that they have been able to obtain both greater employee commitment and more capable managers and employees through their development process. Their UAW-Ford Employee Development and Training Program (EDTP) and Ford's own managerial development process have gone hand-in-hand to help create a more effective organization. Together, these two activities have provided the key ingredient to Ford's more participative culture and their revitalized global competitiveness. First, we will look at their joint educational and training efforts.

Joint Employee Development and Training

Ford and the UAW have developed a unique and comprehensive approach to employee training and development. In 1982, Ford and the UAW created the first ever private-sector, jointly administered employee development and training program. Today it applies to both active and laid-off employees.

Sometimes good things do come out of crisis and this was the case here. The program was initially created through union negotiation when approximately one-half of its peak work force was laid off due to poor economic conditions. UAW and Ford's initial program was designed to help these laid-off employees reorganize their lives and start new careers. In response to this economic crisis, initial activities of the program included sponsoring career-day conferences, vocational planning and interest surveys, career counseling, prepaid tuition assistance, vocational retraining, and job search training.

From its inception, the Employee Development and Training Program (EDTP) was designed to be jointly administered by management and the union. Today, the governing board of EDTP consists of an equal number of members from Ford's Labor Relations Staff and the UAW. If you remember the Horizontal Management Continuum (figure 6–1), you will recall that step V, strategic decision making, is the highest-level delegation of decision making that can occur in an organization. Ford's joint governing board is certainly one of the few to carry the equality in governance this far, and it seems to have paid off handsomely for them in terms of commitment and support from their work force.

The Joint Governing Board sets all policies and approves all program expenditures. Coordination and central administration of EDTP occurs at the Joint National Development and Training Center, located on the campus of Henry Ford Community College in Dearborn, Michigan. It is staffed with both union and company representatives, as well as outside professionals. The Center is funded by a company contribution of five cents per hour worked. It offers seventeen distinct programs, which are based on a survey of employees' needs and wants.

The EDTP training center is the central organization, but it is not the only place where EDTP is administered. Each of Ford's plants has its own EDTP committee. These committees implement employee development activities that meet each location's unique needs, as well as distribute information and directives from the Joint National Development and Training Center.

However significant this EDTP arrangement is in developing employees, Ford stresses that EDTP is not a "stand-alone" program. It is only one of their programs for improving their competitiveness through employee involvement and enhancement.

Ford currently operates development and training to provide lifelong learning that begins with recruitment and selection and continues through retirement. They concentrate on five basic tracks.

- Core company values, policies, and guidelines
- General business, technical, and strategic skills
- Professional/functional knowledge and skills
- Community, governmental, and societal involvement and knowledge
- Individually motivated personal development[10]

These strategic goals are implemented through a variety of specific programs for hourly, salaried and managerial personnel.

EDTP is one of the ways Ford implements their employee and development goals. As already noted, it was created in 1982. It has since been updated and enhanced. Today, as it was in the beginning, EDTP remains *jointly* administered. Both UAW and Ford equally share authority and responsibility for running the program.

EDTP also remains voluntary in nature. At its inception, it was decided that the program would focus on individual choice instead of forcing participation through corporate directives. Participation by local unions, plant officials, and employees is entirely voluntary.

Steps have also been taken to insure EDTP would be able to respond to future as well as current needs. In an effort to take advantage of decentralization, the program is also intended to be responsive to local needs. Ford recognizes that each local facility has different needs, so it established joint local employee development and training program committees. Today, there are five hundred representatives on these committees. Each committee is composed of an equal number of union and management personnel. The Joint National Development and Training Center assists these local employee development committees in identifying the needs of their employees, obtaining necessary resources to conduct their program, and evaluating the results of those local efforts.

The goal was to make training, education, and employee development a comprehensive system that satisfied both active and laid-off employees' needs and desires. Today, their National Center sponsors employee assistance programs designed to help employees solve personal problems. The Center also supports health and safety activities, employee involvement education, and product quality activities. The Center even provides referral services that help employees identify and select the best child care options. Other specialized programs at the Center exist for union leadership and Ford plant management.

Activities for Laid-off Employees. When Ford and the UAW established their joint effort in 1982, the automobile industry was in the middle of a recession. Because of the recession, a number of employees had been laid off. EDTP's early development activities focused on helping these laid-off employees. At that time, there was a serious need for retraining. To that end, EDTP established the Career Services and Reemployment Assistance Center.

It was set up to provide employees with assistance, if needed, whenever Ford was forced to close a facility. In addition to special assistance at plant closings and relocation help, the Center also provided a wide range of other assistance. This included such things as Career Day conferences, career counseling, vocational interest surveys, and job search skills.

Vocational retraining and prepaid tuition (the first of its kind in the United States for laid-off employees) was part of the services. Prepaid tuition made it possible for laid-off employees to return to school on their own. These centers provide comprehensive, one-stop placement and training services. Employees choose their own courses and, depending on their years of seniority at the time of the layoff, could have up to $5,500 in prepaid tuition assistance.

Programs For Active Employees. Since those early times, Ford and their employees' fortunes have turned around. Ford is in the middle of profitable times and the number of laid-off employees using EDTJP's National Center has declined. Ford and the UAW have now refocused their efforts and developed activities for their active employees. This process, referred to as their *Avenues of Employee Growth*, can be seen in figure 12–1.

Each of the options within the Avenue of Employee Growth is a choice each active employee can take toward their own growth and development. This Life and Educational Planning process consists of five separate options. As seen in figure 12–1, these options include:

- Prepaid tuition assistance
- College and university options
- Basic skills enhancement
- Targeted education, training, or counseling
- Successful retirement planning

All of these options are designed to enhance employee professional growth and development as well as improve their personal life. They see those two directly tied together. This comprehensive educational planning for employees also includes the use of professional life education advisors, who provide advice, referral, and support to employees. They have workshops that help employees explore development opportunities. In the few short years of the program's operation, they have counseled more than 12,000 employees. Counseling and workshops are designed to assess a variety of issues about an employee's life and identify methods and resources to help them achieve personal and career goals.

The *prepaid tuition assistance* planning option allows employees a wide variety of training and development courses. Employees have an opportunity to return to school by being provided tuition assistance. Employees can receive prepayment of tuition or other fees up to a maximum of $2,000 per year for credit and degree courses that are selected by employees and approved by management. These courses are designed to improve an employee's growth and development and include courses on communication skills, motivation training, time management, and other areas.

The second avenue of the growth program is the *college and university* option. It is designed to make degree, as well as nondegree, programs more accessible to employees. It includes the following key ingredients:

- A workshop
- Partnership with local educational institutions
- Transfer of credits among partner institutions
- On-site registration and courses at convenient times
- Credits for college level knowledge and skills gained outside the college classroom

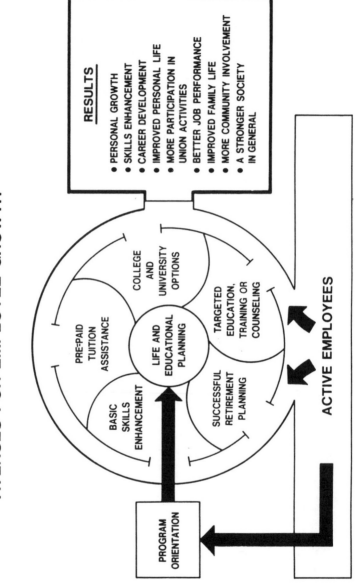

Figure 12–1. UAW-Ford Employee Development and Training Program

Over 120 colleges and universities have become partners with the national centers. In addition, over 50 Ford locations have had on-site classes, which have served over eight thousand employees.

Basic Skills Enhancement

Another innovative option Ford and UAW offer is the *basic skills enhancement* program. This program, like some of the other options available through EDTP, was the first of its kind in the United States. The purpose of it is to help employees upgrade their education and learn new skills. This program is available for displaced, as well as active employees.

This basic skills enhancement option consists of six separate programs. Each of these six programs is designed to help employees upgrade their education or help them improve basic skills (reading, writing, math, English language, communication, etc.). The hope is that such activities will enhance employee self-esteem, self-confidence, and performance both on and off the job.

Employees receive individualized instruction with an open entry/open exit format. Employees decide when to start, stop, or resume their studies. It is competency based, thus encouraging employees to begin at the level they feel comfortable. Educational institutions near local Ford facilities normally supply the teachers and counseling, while the UAW-Ford corporate training center provides supplementary educational services. Employees can also earn high school diplomas through this program.

Ford goes through extensive planning and preparation before they implement their Basic Skills Enhancement program. First, they assess employee needs and desires. Then the results are analyzed and local organizations are contacted to see how to best provide needed services. Next, specific programs are designed for local facilities. The top priority is to identify participants, services, educational procedures, and budgetary concerns. The last step involves actually developing a proposal that is presented to their national headquarters.

Once the proposal has been approved, local facilities are then ready to implement it. This involves recruiting and registering participants. Ford begins their programs by interviewing, testing, and assessing attitudes, interests, and instructional levels. If possible, self-paced learning is used. Progress is monitored and employees are counseled. Records are maintained, and the results of these educational activities are shared between the local and national organizations.

The fourth option available with their Avenues of Growth is the *Targeted Education, Training, or Counseling Projects* option (seen figure 12–1). This option focuses on selecting projects that fit the educational and training needs of specific locations and particular segments of the work force. The program is a supplement to the other options and a means of conducting pilot projects. These pilot projects involve educational, training, or employee development activities where little experience exists. Some past pilot projects range from experiments with developing computer awareness to understanding small-engine repair.

The last Avenue of Growth, as seen in figure 12–1, is the training in *Successful Retirement Planning*. As the name implies, it is designed to help employees and their spouses prepare for retirement. Program activities are usually offered at plant facilities or in their union hall. Training is conducted by both union and company representatives. Subjects include insurance and pension benefits, financial and estate planning, time utilization, travel and recreation, and health and fitness information. It is a complete package designed to empower their employees. But their educational efforts do not stop here.

Ford has also developed complementary educational activities for their professional and technical work force. In fact, their educational and training catalog for salaried employees contains more than three hundred programs. These programs cover whatever is needed, including a wide variety of courses on such subjects as robotics, statistical methods, production engineering, performance management, career assessment, and team-oriented problem solving.[11] All of these activities are in addition to the daily on-the-job training.

So they will not feel left out, Ford also provides their managers with career development at its Executive Development Center. The Center is designed to improve the management skills of its senior executives. Programs are designed to help these managers develop a better understanding of the business. The first program consisted of a five-and-one-half day seminar designed to help managers deal with economic, technological, and human-relations factors. Interaction among different management functions, as well as interaction with different countries and management levels, is encouraged. It is truly an amazing, world-class educational effort.

Concluding Thoughts

Ford and the UAW's joint training was created because of economic and competitive crisis. It is felt that this program was one of the key ingredients to their global competitiveness. At the heart of this training is the broader issue of changing their corporate culture. Ford felt they needed greater employee involvement and a more participative style of management if they were to be competitive.

Most of those at Ford would probably agree that the process of developing employee involvement and creating a more participative management style is becoming more common. They recognize, though, that *all* employees as well as the normal management development and education are at the heart of their ability to continuously improve. It is these development activities that are at the heart of current efforts to reshape their corporate culture.

Ford and their union have recognized that when one change (employee development and choice) occurs, other beneficial changes can occur (employee involvement, teamwork, etc.). This systems approach is even now part of the Executive Training Program. It involves treating business as a network of interdependent processes. This is pure Horizontal Structure thinking.

Things do not change rapidly in highly traditional vertical organizations. Their educational and developmental activities are successful because they have built in a lot of voluntary choices and voluntary agenda. Ford believes this aspect of their development process is essential since employees will feel a greater sense of responsibility and ownership if they have a role in their own educational and developmental efforts.

Certainly a unique aspect of their development activities is that Ford and the UAW downplay the significance of purely quantifiable factors. They say it is important that educational and development efforts have the right to fail—that even failure can be an achievement. Such an attitude helps encourage innovation and experimentation that in turn keeps their developmental efforts on the cutting edge.

Joint employee educational and developmental efforts, like those at Ford, can be a powerful competitive advantage, but its success depends on both management and labor accepting more equitable agreements. At Ford, they call it co-responsibility. Each has to understand the other and accept the legitimacy of the other. Each must see the other as compeer and equal.

Notes

1. "Productivity and Quality Survey," *Focus: Industrial Engineering,* April 1990, p. 6.
2. Bill Smith, "The Motorola Story," In-house publication, p. 11.
3. Peter Drucker, "Workers' Hands Bound by Tradition," *Wall Street Journal,* 2 August 1988, p. 20.
4. Bill Sapority, "The Revolt Against 'Working Smarter,'" *Fortune,* 21 July 1986, p. 59.
5. D. Keith Denton, "Quality is Pepsi's Challenge," *Personnel Journal,* June 1988, p. 143.
6. D. Keith Denton, "Better Management through Budgeting: Instilling a Quality Culture," *Management Review,* October 1988, p. 16.
7. D. Keith Denton, "An Employee Ownership Program That Rebuilt Success," *Personnel Journal,* March 1987, pp. 114–20.
8. Paul A. Banas, "Ford's Transformation: The Role of Employee Involve-

ment and Participative Management," *26th IRC Symposium on Advanced Research in Industrial Relations,* 18 August 1988, pp. 14.

9. Ibid., p. 16.

10. Paul A. Banas, "Worker Retraining: New Skills and Careers," *Ford's Executive Study Conference,* 2–4 December 1987, pp. 3.

11. Ibid., p. 16.

13
Horizontal Motivators

I t seems just about everyone today is talking about empowering their people; yet no one seems to have a clear idea of what they mean by "empower." I assume when managers talk about empowering their people they really mean "How do we get them motivated—you know, charged up about their jobs?" Managers may all agree that in today's market it is essential to have motivated employees, but most still are not sure exactly how to do that. Most would agree that motivating employees has something to do with satisfying their needs and desires.

"Employees can only be motivated when they clearly understand the impact of what they do and they value their part in the service or product they deliver."[1] Those are the words of MaryAnne E. Rasmussen, the vice-president of Worldwide Quality Assurance for American Express's Travel Related Services (TRS). She says that it is pride in one's individual performance that provides every employee with meaning and purpose.[2]

If people do not feel important, if they do not believe they are respected, if they do not have a sense of self-confidence, then nothing else matters. To achieve this there must be a sense of sharing within an organization. There must be a sense of equality and fairness for anyone to feel empowered.

All of us need to believe our jobs are important and to feel that others appreciate our efforts before we can feel a sense of motivation. If managers can help employees feel this way, those employees will take pride in themselves and their work. Rasmussen emphasized this when she said, "There's only one thing that counts in a business—building the self-esteem of your employees. Nothing else matters because what they feel about themselves is what they give to your customers."[3] This may be an oversimplification, but there is a lot of truth in what she says.

As the pyramid flattens and greater responsibility and authority are delegated to lower levels, it seems clear that developing a sense of confidence and self-esteem among all personnel will be essential. The key question remaining is whether to try to simply make employees *feel* important or to actually bring them into the decision-making process and let them *be* important.

Both approaches can be an effective way of providing people with a sense of importance and self-confidence, but only one way creates perpetual energy within an organization. Trying to keep people motivated through communication or recognition is a constant battle. It is often an auxiliary or add-on approach in that it takes a continuous effort to keep employees motivated and excited about what they do, but requires no fundamental organizational change.

Motivation does not have to be that way. Motivation can be created automatically by structurally rearranging the way organizations are run and how decisions are made, a structural or horizontal approach, or through incentives, under an auxiliary or vertical motivation approach. An excellent example of effective vertical motivation is seen in the case of American Express.

Vertical Motivation

American Express has used incentives just about as well as anyone could. They have over one hundred measures of customer service alone. Those measures are evaluated, reported, reviewed and, analyzed on a monthly basis. American Express sets benchmarks, and the results are shared with all their employees so they can see both individual and team performances.

One of their best-known motivators is their "Great Performer Award." This awards is given to honor their employees around the world who went above and beyond the call of duty. In 1987 one of these top awards went to an employee in Salt Lake City who spoke in German to an upset Dutch tourist who spoke no English. She had been robbed, and the employee not only refunded her traveler's checks, but also helped her get a new passport and airline tickets issued so she could get home. Winners of these Great Performers Awards are flown to New York, wined, dined, given cash awards, and are featured at a banquet attended by American Express's top executives.

Although recognition is important, by itself it is not enough to develop the self-confidence and esteem needed. Because of this, American Express spends time communicating with and updating employees about what is going on in the company, including new activities, new products, new quality initiatives, and their competitor's strategies. The company provides a report on the previous year's accomplishments and upcoming goals and plans. They also make extensive use of employee newsletters, videotapes, and teleconferences. The objective is to keep employees informed and motivated.

American Express does a very good job of recognizing and communicating with their employees. They believe that people want to do a good job and it is the manager's job to encourage them. Their vertical approach to motivation is based on the belief that people do things because they are conditioned to, that human behavior is modified or shaped by stimulus, response, and reinforcement. Motivation is thus a matter of attention to rewards and incentives.

There are a variety of vertical motivation tools available and in use. These can either be categorized as employee recognition methods like those used by American Express where performance is measured against a standard and beating the standard is rewarded, or as a variety of vertical motivational techniques all of which entail some form of "communicating."

It is not hard to determine when communication is being used strictly to motivate. For instance, Management By Walking Around (MBWA), made so popular by innovative companies like Hewlett-Packard, is often simply another vertical motivational tool. If a manager simply walks around and listens to his or her people, then it is a vertical use of MBWA. If it is used to show employees that their opinions are important, it is still vertical motivation. If it is used mainly to keep close ties to subordinates, it is still vertical motivation. However, if MBWA is used to change the way decisions are made, then it is a horizontal motivational tool.

As seen in figure 13–1, the philosophy and techniques for vertical and horizontal motivation differ based on how they are used. Horizontal motivation occurs whenever there is an *essential* structural change within an organization or department where power, decision-making authority, and responsibility are actually redistributed. Profit sharing is one technique that can be either a horizontal or vertical tool depending on how it is used. If employees really do have a say in designing the profit-sharing program, it is horizontal; otherwise, it is vertical.

While profit sharing can fall either way, many techniques are clearly designed to just show employees how important they are, but not to actually increase their relative importance in the structure of the organization. Most employee communication falls in this vertical motivation category. When someone asks for another's "input," they are often simply seeking opinions without the intention of involving the employee in the decision-making process directly. Things like "open door" policies or "brown bag" lunches, where the CEO and other higher-ups rub shoulders with those at the lowest level within the organization, are typical vertical examples.

Other vertical motivation tools include the use of employee newsletters that are designed to increase the visibility of employee contributions to the corporation. Videotapes and teleconferences that inform rather than being used for real decision making are other such cases.

	Auxiliary Vertical Motivators	Structural Horizontal Motivators
Philosophy	Recognition Eliminating "symbolic" status symbols between levels in organizations Measuring performance and rewarding people Open communication to increase visibility of employees' contribution	Creating greater equity and fairness Eliminating real differences between levels within an organization Delegating duties to lower levels Decentralization and participative management with decision making authority
Techniques	Sharing of good management practices Shortening the communication distances between levels of management Employee suggestion programs (without decision-making ability) Profit sharing (without direct influence or organization choices) Quality Circles Network Teams (without decision-making capacity)	SPC (Step 1) JIT (Step 2) "Line-of-sight" teams (Step 2) Cross-training (Steps 1–5) TQC (Steps 1–5) NOAC (if lines of authorit change) (Steps 1–5) ESOP (Steps 4–5) Stock options (Steps 1–5) Progit sharing (with decision making) (Step 5) Structure teams (Steps 1–5)
Examples	Hewlett-Packard's MBWA Ford's Mutual Growth Forum Federal Express "brown bag" lunches with troops G. E.'s transfer of good management practices	Hewlett-Packard's flextime (Step 1) Ford's joint training efforts (Step 5) SRC commodity budgets (Step 5) Pepsi's stock options

Figure 13–1. Vertical and Horizontal Motivation Compared

Undoubtedly, vertical motivation techniques and approaches will continue to be used. They are the easiest and most risk-free approaches to motivation, but it is becoming increasingly clear that the real competitive advantage will come when we change the way management decisions are made. It will take something beyond simple recognition for a job well done or communicating and sharing information about goals and accomplishments for business to create the dynamic energy needed to survive.

Horizontal Motivation

As long as a large section of the work force feels second class, the organization remains vulnerable. CEOs and other people with power never have trouble feeling "involved." It is those without power, influence, and status who feel powerless and apathetic.

Greater equality within the workplace is such a competitive advantage that many companies consider its implementation proprietary information. Whenever corporations take steps toward this equality, they enhance their overall competitiveness. Some companies recognized the advantage of equality early on.

As early as 1958 IBM eliminated hourly wages and put everyone in IBM on straight salary. That move eliminated one of the major distinctions between white-and blue-collar employees.[4] These tentative first steps toward creating greater equality are essential if motivation is to be self-sustaining, rather than something that has to be artificially created through incentives and rewards.

When Japanese firms have their managers and employees wear the same uniform, they are—at least symbolically—acknowledging the equality between employees and management. Federal Express's and Delta Airline's no-furlough policies make equality more of a reality. Delegating managerial duties down to teams of employees is acknowledging the ability of employees to do what used to be thought of as exclusively managerial activities. Ford's joint training effort with the U.A.W. is the ultimate sign of respect. At Ford management actually shares authority with their union. This is a fundamental change in the way decisions were made. This is much more than evaluating performance, selecting employees for special recognition, and allowing workers to make recommendations; this is a solid beginning to eliminating the distinction between employer and employee.

Team management where members make line-of-sight decisions is another example of using a horizontal management tool. Concurrent engineering and production and process teams responsible for the whole decision-making process also represent structural changes horizontal in nature. However, not all such teams are truly horizontally structured. If teams are used simply to investigate problems, identify choices, and make recommendations, then they are vertical motivational devices. The same thing could be said for the quality-of-work-life programs that were popular in the 1980s. Most were simply vertical motivational tools because they produced no change in decision making.

Horizontal Problem Solving

Some programs and processes automatically change the way decisions are made. These methods of production and organization cannot be "subverted." SPC is an excellent example of this. SPC relies on workers using statistical control charts and sampling plans rather than on quality control inspection departments to do all the inspection for receiving, inprocessing, and shipping. Employees, rather than staff inspectors, track their own performance, and employees, rather than the inspection department, identify what is in control or out of control. Like any truly horizontal motivator, SPC requires the granting of more authority, control, and decision making to lower levels.

Another popular concept mentioned at the first of the book, Total Quality Management (TQM), makes use of SPC, but is broader in nature and also entails even greater use of employee decision making. TQM's goal is to produce products of high quality in the first place rather than finding defects in products through inspection. Everyone involved in producing and delivering the product is trained in both SPC and broader SPC concepts.

TQM involves the improvement of the basic product and service design and developing close relationships with suppliers. Most importantly though, it requires that every worker on the assembly line and in the warehouse, as well as those that pack or ship the basic product continually monitor and improve the quality of their work. Responsibility to improve quality does not rest with inspection; it rests with those that produce the products or provide the services. Quality and daily problem solving is, thus, a line, not a staff, function. Delegating greater control of quality to lower levels is a vital part of TQM and, when properly applied, an excellent example of a horizontal motivator.

If an organization has poor human relations, then it might as well forget implementing TQM. Authoritarian or highly vertical organizations trying to implement horizontal management approaches like TQM often fail. Managers in these companies want to improve quality, but do not want to go through the work of streamlining the organization and empowering people.

The same shortsighted attitude has short-circuited many JIT efforts. JIT as a "pull" inventory system is a sharp contrast to the normal inventory methods. Normally, as products are assembled, partially completed subassemblies, parts, components, and related work-in-process (WIP) inventory is pushed from one center to the next.

Bottlenecks and backlogs occur when some work centers in the assembly area move more slowly than others. JIT takes the approach that work centers downstream (internal customers) control the pace of work, not the ones upstream (suppliers) as they do in the push system.

JIT requires rethinking the production process, but it is becoming widely used in repetitive types of operations. JIT not only dramatically reduces inventory, but also changes relationships between management and labor. JIT cannot be practical without changes in how work is managed. Implementing it usually requires changing the layout of the plant, criteria of supplier selection, methods of scheduling, and the training of employee's. It requires cross-training so people can do a variety of tasks. It requires good quality, good maintenance, accuracy, and excellent communication. Most of all, it requires giving more power to the operational level because the workers themselves are responsible for producing perfect products with no scrap, no excess inventory, no mistakes, and no miscalculations. Each worker must have a great deal more decision-making responsibility in the JIT production mode.

Normally when using JIT (sometimes called stockless production or zero inventory), process inventory is drastically reduced. In this system, production is stopped until any production or quality problem is solved. For instance, if a downstream user or customer detects a quality problem, production is immediately halted until the problem is found and corrected. In theory, the problem is solved on the line immediately by employees and management.

Other EDM Motivators

JIT is not the only Employee Decision Making (EDM) motivator. American Airline's highly successful Quality of Work Life (QWL) process is another case. R. L. Crandall, chairman and president of American Airlines, said, "We started with the idea that many workplace problems can be solved most effectively from the bottom up, instead of from the top down. That's a reversal of the way a lot of folks have thought for a long time and it took some getting used to."[5]

EDM goes by many names: QWL, JIT, QC Circles, and so forth. Regardless of the name, it is essential not only that employees be involved, but they must also be part of both problem-solving and decision-making processes. This is in contrast to Employee Involvement (EI), which, as practiced by many managers, is really a vertical motivator since it is used only to improve communication or recognize employee contributions. EI can even involve employees in investigating, analyzing, and proposing solutions, but until employees actually have decision-making authority, EI cannot be classified as a horizontal motivator.

One example of where EDM is used is Byerly's grocery stores. Byerly's is a highly successful and very decentralized chain of grocery stores located in Minneapolis, Minnesota. The general manager of each Byerly's store sets his or her own prices and chooses which products will be sold based on perceived needs of the area. Decentralization extends all the way to the departments within each store. For instance, those running each store's produce department do their own buying, pricing, and hiring.

Each of the Byerly's supermarkets are essentially autonomous and do not simply parrot the buying policies of the corporate headquarters. Each store follows guidelines, but those guidelines do not involve specific products. Corporate management does not track performance in detail because no two store's are exactly alike.

Nordstrom, an upscale West Coast retailer, also maintains a highly decentralized system. Departments, stores, and regional managers are free to make their own decisions. Likewise, each region has its own buyers to insure that it caters to local tastes.

Degrees

Decentralization comes in many degrees. It can be thought of as steps toward horizontal management (see figure 6–1). Step I could involve the use of flextime. Hewlett-Packard makes wide use of flextime. Under their plan, there is a "window" for starting work of about two hours, say between 6:30 A.M. and 8:30 A.M. Employees must put in their eight hours, but the specific arrangement is left up to the employees. At Hewlett-Packard, the system is self-policing because employees working less than eight hours must contend with peer-group disapproval.

Federal Express uses a similar flextime plan except the window is much smaller. Employees have a ten-minute leeway. If they want, they can arrive ten minutes before a shift begins and then leave ten minutes early. It is a matter of degrees, but they still have some managerial-level decision making.

One company that uses decentralization to a great degree is Rochester Products in Coopersville, Michigan. They make fuel injectors for General Motors. The company has a policy of soliciting advice from workers about who should be promoted. The company also asks them for help in evaluating potential suppliers.[6] It is hard to say if real decision making is allocated to these workers or if their input is simply being sought. If they are simply soliciting advice, it is only a vertical motivation technique (though a very effective one). If they actually have a say in the choices made, then it is a horizontal motivator.

There is no doubt that employees at Kodak's Precision Component Manufacturing Division in Rochester, New York, are actively making decisions at step II. These assembly workers, who make X-ray cassettes and cartons for Kodak film, arrange their own hours, keep track of their productivity, and repair their own machines.[7] Some team members even go beyond step II (see Horizontal Continuum, figure 6–1), and actually teach fellow members SPC, meet with suppliers, interview prospective recruits, and help manage JIT inventory.

Ownership

Horizontal motivation occurs most easily when employees are given a sense of ownership: a feeling that they have a personal stake in the success of some operation or the business. Store managers at Wal-Mart have such a stake. They can keep up to ten percent of their store's pre-tax profit. Some store managers earn more than $100,000 in salary and bonuses. That is ownership; assuming, as figure 6–1 shows, that real decision making occurs. Do these employees make decisions that directly affect their profit sharing? If so, then this is horizontal organization in action.

Employees are encouraged to purchase company stock. Wal-Mart provides an incentive to do so by contributing up to 15 percent of the cost and paying the brokerage fee. The result is that 8 percent of the company's stock is employee owned. If an employee works one thousand hours a year and has been employed with them for two years, Wal-Mart will contribute a percentage of the employee's wages to a profit-sharing trust. In 1983, it was 8.4 percent. It has not been uncommon for hourly employees to retire with over $100,000 in profit-sharing distributions.

Ownership does not have to come purely through financial means. The department heads, who are strictly hourly employees and manage one of each store's thirty departments (e.g. sporting goods, electronics, etc.), have access to financial information that many companies would never show a general manager, this includes data on costs, freight charges, and profit margins.

Future Trends

Ownership plans have obvious advantages and many have been around for years. Hewlett-Packard established an employee stock purchase plan with a 25 percent subsidy from the company decades ago. Employee Stock Ownership Plans (ESOPs) are another popular ownership plan. ESOPs are constantly changing, but perhaps Brunswick Corporation's approach might be the wave of the future.

In 1983 Brunswick began granting employees stock every year at no cost. When Brunswick started, they received a tax credit, but when the tax credit ended, they kept the ESOP in effect, taking the cost of the stock right out of earnings. They are only one of a few to do that. Six years after its inception, employees who had been with the company during those years had earned 150 shares of Brunswick stock worth $2,500.

What makes Brunswick's ESOP so unique is the simple *equity* of it. Rather than a few "fat cat" managers receiving a disappropriate share, it is far more equitable. At Brunswick every employee in a given operating division receives the same amount of stock, based upon the division's performance, regardless of his or her salary line.

The philosophy is summed up by their chairman, Jack F. Reichert, who said the two most important factors in keeping employees satisfied are ownership and trust. If employees feel that they can trust management and have ownership in the business, they will work harder to achieve goals. He also said that employees "don't hurt what they feel they own." Another way to do this is through stock options.

Stock Options

As the name implies, stock options mean that corporate personnel being offered options or opportunities to purchase company stock. In the past it has been both a powerful incentive and a status symbol. When the company awarded you stock options, it meant you had made it: you were a member of the elite. Robert Ochsner, director of compensation for Hay Management Consultants, said, "The average company may have its top 300 to 400 executives in a (stock option) program, up from 100 executives 10 years ago."[8] Towers Perrin, a consulting firm, surveyed two hundred major companies in 1988 and found that only 7 percent offered stock options to more than ten percent of their employees, and none to more than 35 percent of their workers.[9]

PepsiCo broke this tradition and began offering stock options to the 100,000 full-time employees of Pizza Hut, Kentucky Fried Chicken, Taco Bell, Pepsi-Cola, and Frito-Lay in 1989. In the process they may have created a competitive advantage. At the very least, they have reduced the status barriers between organizational levels and created a horizontal motivator. PepsiCo is using the stock option plan they call "SharePower" to build a sense of empowerment, ownership, and commitment among participants.

How It Started. PepsiCo chairman and CEO, Wayne Calloway, challenged his staff to come up with a way to give all employees a sense of empowerment and ownership. Initially, they evaluated various forms of ESOPs, but they felt these were basically entitlement programs and not motivational. They would not involve any real decision making. In figure 13–1 ESOPs are listed as a horizontal motivator, but this assumes employees actually do have a say in financial (step IV) and strategic (step V) decisions. If they are used for some other purpose, they are vertical motivators.

PepsiCo felt that ESOPs, as they were being used, were not motivating employees, so Charlie Rogers, PepsiCo's vice-president of Compensation and Benefits, came up with the idea of stock options for the employees. He and his staff investigated the details and set up the program. PepsiCo feels that these options create a sense of ownership for employees, and is appealing to shareholders because it only rewards employees when shareholders' value is created.

How It Works. Under the SharePower plan, the company plans that at the beginning of July every year employees will be granted options totaling ten percent of their compensation (including bonuses, commissions, and overtime) for the previous calendar year. These options give employees the right to buy company stock within the next ten years at the 1 July price. Each grant vests at 20 percent per year, so after five years it becomes fully vested. Employees may purchase the shares at the option price, or if they do not need to have the cash in hand to make those purchases, they can apply the stock's appreciation to the purchases of new shares.

Stock options can significantly affect an employee's financial well-being. PepsiCo notes that an employee making $30,000 a year could accumulate $387,000 during a thirty-year career if he or she held on to their shares and the stock's growth rate was ten percent. If the stock were to grow at 15 percent as it has over the last fourteen years, the same employee could accumulate $1.2 million during the same period.

Under PepsiCo's stock-option plan, employees could benefit from the appreciation of approximately $200 million worth of stock each year, but there is no guarantee of anything. Employees, like stockholders, receive no benefits when the stock does not appreciate. The stock-option plan creates greater equity between lower and upper levels. In turn, PepsiCo hopes it will motivate employees to think and act like owners since they benefit directly from increasing the value of their stock options.

It is the same type of logic applied to ESOPs, but PepsiCo believes their stock options provide employees a stronger sense of ownership than ESOPs, for ESOPs can be created to avoid takeovers or for tax and financial reasons. ESOPs sometimes even require that employees exchange existing benefits for increased employee stock ownership. PepsiCo's Share-Power Plan was entirely additive; nothing has been taken away.

Their stock option plan's key benefit from a motivational view was adeptly summarized by Michael MacCoby, a management consultant in Washington, D.C., who said, "Anything that gives ordinary workers some of the same benefits as the top managers increases the sense of being part of a common enterprise."[10] This does not make them compeers yet, but such a program does create a sense of equity and fairness by eliminating the real or perceived differences in status, pay, and privileges within an organization and that is the very definition of horizontal motivation.

Concluding Thoughts

People are motivated to work for many reasons. There is no universal motivator. It depends on the situation, on the people, and on what is important to them. A lot of managers recognize the need to involve their people. It is obvious too that much of this motivation is occurring at random. That is unfortunate since we lose much of the long-term value of motivation when it is not conducted in a coherent manner or targeted toward clearly defined goals.

It is pretty clear from reading the literature and listening to practitioners that these same practitioners recognize the need to provide better products and services to their customers. They generally recognize the need to better meet their customers' needs and desires. Likewise, most of these managers recognize that it is their people who will be the key to doing this. However, many of their efforts are doomed to failure unless they first recognize exactly what it is that they want to do, then decide how they want to go about doing it.

It takes real forethought and considerable effort to sit down in the middle of day-to-day crises and decide what one wants to accomplish. Most just know things need to change. They *wish* people would care more about what they do. They feel that they should do something but just do not have the time to approach the situations logically and rationally.

Ask yourself whether you want employee input, communication, and recommendations (in other words, involvement), if you want real, significant changes in the way the organization is run. If you want real change, rather than greater involvement, you really may be wanting greater lower-level control and ownership of problems and decisions.

Do you believe that employees and those at lower levels really do know and can manage their jobs better and can make intelligent decisions? If so, then you will want to create a step I (on the horizontal continuum) organization. On the other hand, do you believe that groups or teams of people, rather than first-line supervisors, can better manage daily work activities (e.g. scheduling, hiring, firing, rewarding each other)? If this is the case, you will want to set up a step II organization.

Even further along the continuum, do you believe that given enough time, training, and technology, lower levels can take over intermediate or long-range managerial planning, organizing, and controlling efforts? If so, then a step III organization is possible. Finally, if you believe that given enough effort, even corporate-wide financial and strategic issues can be delegated to lower and lower levels, then a step IV or V organization is possible for you.

In all of these cases, it takes congruent perception, commitment, and motivation tools. Horizontal motivation can be aimed at steps I through V. Each motivational effort can produce greater empowerment if perception and commitment are involved. Each motivational effort can be a part of a transition from one phase to the next. First, each motivator has to: (1) recognize what changes are needed, (2) have a desire to change, and (3) know how to change. Knowing how to change is the hard part because there are no simple rules, no one-minute manager approaches that are going to help. What will help is deciding how you want to structure your organization. Begin by asking yourself the following questions:

• Do I want to maintain my vertical organization or to implement a more horizontal approach?

• What step (I through V) horizontal organization do I think is appropriate (based on my current level of training and technology and other factors) for my company?

• What groups of employees will participate (will it be a partial or full conversion to a particular horizontal organization)?

• Which horizontal motivators are appropriate to my situation?

Notes

1. MaryAnne E. Rasmussen, "American Express Quality Culture: Our Key To Motivating Employees," *American Productivity and Quality Center Executive Conference*, Cambridge, Massachusetts, 4 August, 1988, p. 3.

2. Ibid., p. 3.

3. Ibid., p. 3.

4. Thomas J. Watson, *A Business and Its Beliefs* (New York, N.Y.: Mc-Graw-Hill, 1963), p. 54.

5. R. L. Crandall, Speech at Statewide Quality of Work Life Seminar, 16 May, 1977.

6. Jeremy Main, "The Winning Organization," *Fortune*, 26 September, 1988, p. 60.

7. Ronald Henkoff, "Cutting Cost: How To Do It Right," *Fortune*, 9 April, 1990, p. 48.

8. Jolie Solomon, "Pepsi Offers Stock Options To All Not Just Honchos," *The Wall Street Journal*, 28 June, 1989, p. B1.

9. Ibid., p. B1.

10. Ibid., p. B1.

14
Dealing with Short Ladders

T he subject of the previous chapter was motivation. Motivation, or the lack of it, is also the reason that many CEO directives concerning restructuring fail to realize their potential. Specifically, it is middle-and lower-level management's lack of motivation and their resistance to change that scuttles many upper-management initiatives. The reason for this resistance was noted by Richard Dotlich, a vice-president of Human Resources at Honeywell, who said, "Management still assumes its role is to tell and not tell. Information is power, and access to it remains a clear badge of rank to managers. Even though many companies are forcing managers to put out information on the number of units produced, cost and other sensitive issued, the idea still doesn't set right."[1] The same can be said of efforts to create a more equitable organization. If horizontal management is to be implemented successfully, it must have the full enthusiastic support of middle-and lower-level managers.

So Where Is Up?

As organizations grow flatter, many operational people openly embrace the possibility of increased responsibility, autonomy, and authority. However, many competent people will resist flat organizations because they see them as a threat. What of the corporate fast trackers—the rising stars? Where do they go? How do they get ahead? How will they grow and develop when career ladders become a great deal shorter than they are today? What do you do when there is no "up" and no way to get anywhere?

Flat organizations may have a more effective structure. They may be more competitive in theory, but until they address these concerns, little real change will occur. Potential benefits of flatter organizations will not be reached until management is able to keep their most aggressive, most career-minded, most upwardly mobile people motivated.

Greater power and equity at the lower levels and throughout the organization is often feared and resented. When we tell everyone to start dressing alike, to stop wearing red ties and become team players, many star players will revolt. If they do not revolt, at least they will express open resistance and resentment.

This type of situation has been played out frequently in years past. Upper managers decide that they want to develop a more participative culture. But then plans are never realized because middle managers and supervisors feel threatened. After all, it is they who will need to share power and learn to coach rather than manage.

Not only must these people share, but their time between promotions will be extended dramatically. These talented, capable, and skilled people are already beginning to wait. David Rhodes of the consulting firm, Towers Perrin, says, "When companies flatten organizations, that limits the number of rungs on the ladder, which lengthens the time between promotions."[2] Ask yourself the same question: Would you wait years for a promotion rather than months?

Rhode's comments appeared in a *Fortune* magazine article that examined the frustrations that many already face in an organizational world where flat is fashionable but extremely frustrating to those used to getting promotions, perks, and power. The article relayed many such stories. The case of Susan Doten, a director of marketing in Quaker Oats's pet-food division, was fairly typical. At thirty one, she had moved quickly through six jobs in nine years, but as the corporate pyramid flattened she noted, "I will hang out at this level for a lot longer than I hung out at the lower levels. There are about thirteen marketing directors in the U.S. grocery products, then only four vice-presidents of marketing at the next level."[3]

Ms. Doten's experience is not and will not be unique. Rhodes predicts that "by the year 2000 the typical large corporation will have half the management levels and one-third the managers that it has today."[4] Imagine what will happen when the baby boomers hit this bottleneck. So it is not simply a problem for fast trackers; everyone is going to be affected. What is the reason for achieving when there is no place to go!

Zigzag

One of a series of solutions may have been invented by those who are already faced with a flat organization. What happens when you cannot move up? You move laterally. It is a move favored by Doten of Quaker Oats. She says she may eventually have to move to another area to "grow herself."

It appears that organizations, especially flat ones, are going to need generalists rather than specialists to manage increasingly diverse responsibilities. Surely the day of the specialist is coming to an end, and it is in direct proportion to the growth of flatter organizations. For many in these circumstances the way to get ahead is not straight up, but sideways.

Anne Pol of Pitney Bowes was in a senior position in the human-resources area. She needed operating experience, so she moved laterally to run a plant. Later, she came back to a top position in the personnel job at corporate headquarters. Next, she plans to go over to another job in operations. Why would she seem to be making these zigzag moves? She says, "It's been obvious that lateral moves are necessary if you want to progress up the corporate ladder."[5]

Lateral moves have been effective in the development of some of our best executives. Why not make it essential to progression? It is not only an astute career move for those on the move, it is actually extremely good for the corporation as a whole. Clearly, one of the themes of successful companies like Glaxo, SRC, Pepsi General Bottlers, and many others is that we are going to need people who are ready for success. Success means having both breadth and depth.

This cross-training could occur by implementing some form of managerial job rotation. At SRC, one manager started out as a clerk and moved throughout the entire organization from accounting to production to marketing and sales. This company continuously encourages people to switch assignments. The reason is to help them learn new jobs and to allow them to teach others their job. It is often said that only when you can teach others, do you really learn the job for the first time. It also helps when everyone is focused on the corporation rather than on a particular discipline—as is common in inefficient organizations.

Steps without Ladders

Just because organizations are flat does not mean there should not be a sense of achievement. Even flat organizations can have steps. One company that has faced the problem with short ladders and come up with some solutions is Texas Instruments (TI). In early 1989, Kenneth V. Spenser, vice-president in charge of TI's worldwide industrial control business, told 240 managers and supervisors at TI's Johnson City, Tennessee, operation that things had to change.

At the time of his speech there were eight layers of organization. He explained why they needed a flatter organization and what the benefits would be. This included the fact that with eight layers they were spending a great deal of time on internal problems and internal communication. He explained that with a flatter organization, people would focus more on external communications. As you might expect, most people at the meeting thought a flatter organization was a great idea. The mood changed when he said that the next time they had a meeting, it would not be held in their current room but rather in their mini-auditorium, which was much smaller.[6]

Imagine the reaction—stunned silence. Everyone knew what that meant and, in fact, by late 1989 their supervisory and managerial team was down to 103 people. The number of organizational layers had been trimmed from eight to four. Spenser himself used to have only four people reporting to him; now he had fourteen people. He emphasized that management needed to peel away management layers starting from the top rather than from the bottom.[7]

So how did they do it? Surprisingly, not in the heavy-handed manner one might first imagine. Most of those displaced managers simply returned to their old disciplines. The interesting thing is that they did it without sacrificing the chance of career advancement. TI had introduced a new concept, the "technical ladder."

As a result of this process, TI achieved greater efficiency while avoiding the slump in morale commonly associated with restructuring. In their restructuring they sought to eliminate excess, inefficient work. To do that, they focused on their management structure, which in 1988 included the use of two hundred "cost centers." Often the centers were present in part because "one criterion for determining career progress was whether or not an individual headed a cost center."[8]

Kenneth Spenser realized that these cost centers added little value to the organization. What they did do was create excessive paperwork with activities like forecasting, reconciling, and reviewing costs. About 20 percent of the manager's time in one of these cost centers was spent on supervisory matters. The remaining 80 percent was spent on technical work. He emphasized that after restructuring the managers who remained spent more of their time motivating, communicating, and doing other managerial activities.

What of those who were "left in the dust?" They were not demoted; instead, the corporation just changed the rules. As noted, many former managers simply returned to their former disciplines, such as engineering and other technical fields. Most importantly, they still have a chance for advancement through TI's technical ladder.

Technical Ladders

At the Johnson City plant, their technical ladder now has eight rungs, but without the drawbacks of their eight-layer bureaucracy. The progression for one on the technical ladder is "junior position, associate engineer, engineer, senior engineer, master engineer, member of the group technical staff, fellow and senior fellow."

"Senior fellow is a position right next to God," Mr. Spenser quips.[9] TI's experience makes an important point. When status is taken away, it must be returned somehow. At TI, they not only lowered the rungs on their technical ladder, they also created more rungs, and they made it worthwhile to climb those rungs rather than trying to become a traditional manager. If people want status, they now have another direction to go. They changed the way people perceived technical positions. For instance, at the top of the technical ladder, a professional can make as much money as any vice-president in the corporation.

Dual-track compensation, which involves paying nonmanagerial professionals on a par with managers, is a simple but effective solution to at least part of the status problem. Those that implement this process realize that the manager group is no better than others. As in TI's case, managing a profit center is not the only way to get to the top. Just because you have a flat organization does not necessarily mean people will plateau or peak early. The result of TI's restructuring was impressive. They increased sales and profits with sales going up by 17 percent, while reducing cost by 15 percent.

Stretching and Status

Their success is encouraging, but the fact that their restructuring worked should not seem that unusual. A model already exists in the academic field. In universities, teachers can get promoted from instructor to assistant professor to associate professor and eventually to full professor. Most people on campus believe that the best is a full, tenured professor—not a department head, not a dean, not a vice-president, not even the president. The "plum" of all the jobs for many would be a "distinguished professor," a position analogous to a senior fellow at TI.

Privileges and respect determine status. Given enough perks, any organization can emphasize whatever track they think is essential. Certainly it is possible as well as wise to keep many people in technical slots rather than always requiring that advancement be through managerial avenues.

In fact, many people have trouble changing from a technical to a managerial career. There are highly capable technicians, engineers, and other professionals simply cannot adapt to the new skills needed to be a manager of people. It is a simple fact that some technical people should remain technical and never be a manager of people. Under TI's new structure the error of thinking that there is anything wrong with that has been corrected. Allowing more earning power to a technician or specialist can help eliminate the sense of being stuck that many feel in a flat organization. Adding challenges within disciplines and stretching the ability of people in those positions (like the use of SRC's commodity budgets) can also reduce the sense of being stuck.

As in TI's case, restructuring can be a win-win situation where a series of skills and responsibilities can be gradually added within a discipline. Why should a technician have to become a traditional manager in order to feel a sense of growth? It does not make sense. When technical or specialized jobs (e.g. accounting, engineering, etc.) are expanded, then you let people know how they can get from one point to the next. Along the way, make sure enough coaching and training are available so the growth occurs in the right way.

This growth can occur in a variety of ways, including cross-training similar to that used by SRC. It can occur by stretching jobs, adding new responsibilities and challenges. Some of these activities include participating in projects and problem-solving teams or other temporary assignments. It could also involve more specialized or advanced training in other fields like human resources, computers or other areas.

Beyond Cross-training and Stretching

The previous discussion centered around how to emphasize promotions and perks in flat organizations. Sometimes it seems that is all organizations focus on. The question remains, "Why should promotions or perks be the only reward or indication of one's success?" Up should not be the only way to be successful. Many may give lip service to the concept of equity, but the proof is in the perks. Are there differences in the dining room, parking places, desk size, number of windows, or thickness of carpet between employees and managers? It seems absurd from the outside, but it is a fact of life that many consider such "badges" important. Such people seem to need a way of saying, "I've made it *and you haven't*."

Evidence of this can be found in the circumstances surrounding the savings and loan crisis. Thomas Spegel, former head of Columbia Savings and Loan of Beverly Hills, California, allegedly squandered depositors' money on air travel, vacation homes, and rock concert tickets.[10] Other questionable expenditures included limousine service, luxurious private dining rooms, and corporate jets. Another head of a failed savings and loan entertained politicians on a $7 million yacht maintained at corporate expense and used corporate funds to pay for $13.2 million for a Rubens painting he hung in his living room.[11]

Such abuses are not peculiar to the savings and loan industry. Remember earlier in the book that Socrates had suggested the highest-paid person in a community should not be paid more than five times as much as the lowest-paid one. Imagine what he would have thought of the disparity of some of today's corporations. Berkley professor Graef S. Crystal observes that the gap between long tenure and hourly workers and that of the pay of CEOs is ever widening. Typically, CEOs earn 130 times the average U.S. factory worker's annual salary of $21,735, versus 34 times as much fourteen years ago.[12] Some CEOs earn far beyond that. Richard Eamers, CEO of National Medical Enterprises, is paid 625 times as much as the lowest-paid worker in his company. Is there any doubt that employees sometimes doubt management's sincerity?

Things Change

There has been an incredible amount of conspicuous consumption, but things are changing. The Japanese automakers are renowned for eliminating status barriers. In some corporations, everyone dresses alike and eats in the same cafeteria. In some firms, like SRC, the upper managers "shoot pool" and socialize with their blue-collar employees. The corporate headquarters and offices are a relatively spartan environment. Until this issue of perks and privileges is addressed, many operational personnel will continue to feel like second-class citizens. For some, it is a constant putdown. For others, it excites greed and envy. It corrupts the reasons to move up.

There are other approaches that can be effective. The use of technical ladders and incentives like pay for skills or knowledge can be a more valuable goal to pursue. Rather than pursuing perks and privileges, encourage learning and participation in problem solving as rewards. Reward managers for "growing" and developing others. Provide mentors and role models to others. Provide status and recognition for those mentors. We do not need a philosopher king, but perhaps we need philosopher managers.

Given a chance, many people will choose equity over perks and power. Henry do Montebello of the executive search firm, Russell Reynolds Associates, says, "People will take extraordinary risks in their careers for equity."[13] There are a variety of choices available and corporate America has spent too much time making power plays and breeding a long session of greedy, shortsighted piranha in search of their next status reward.

No wonder corporate cultures can be so divisive, political, and counterproductive. When you think about it, would you rather work with those seeking equity and fairness or those seeking power, position, perks, and privileges? We cannot blame people if they are this way. It is the system they function in that makes them like this. We can create a more harmonious corporate climate if we are careful about which behaviors we reward. It should be obvious that corporate climates based on rewarding those managers who nurture and teach, and who are compensated on the basis of the learning, knowledge, and problem-solving skills they display are far better than ones that encourage status seeking and privilege.

Dynamic Motivation

An example of a healthy attitude toward work was demonstrated by Jawahar S. Sawardeker, vice-president of Technical Affairs for Glaxo America (discussed in Chapter 11). He was describing his company and was
asked how they keep their people involved and productive when it can
mean eliminating one's job. He said when their people work on a task
force to improve productivity or on continuous-improvement projects, in
fact they might end up eliminating their own jobs. Many might fear loss
of employment and therefore might not be productive. So what do they
do?

Sawardeker responded by saying that it is not a problem because
Glaxo employees never have to worry about that. In fact, at Glaxo a successful manager should be able to phase himself out of a job and move on
to something else. He has been told that he should be able to move on in
about two years and is constantly at work phasing out his current job.

Sawardeker believes that we should all be phasing out our jobs. In
dynamic organizations we should be able to move into other jobs, not
necessarily up. He says his corporation is constantly looking for people
who can phase themselves out of a job. This is not a worry for him; there
are a lot of other good jobs waiting for him within the organization.

Perhaps that is the way organizations ought to be designed. No permanent titles, only project directors and continuously reforming teams and
task forces. Each is thereby guaranteed temporary work on a permanent
basis. Compared to such a system the vertical organization seems obsolete
and dysfunctional.

It is conceivable that completely horizontal organizations will resemble these teams or cells of individuals brought together to resolve temporary problems and opportunities. Such structure, or lack of structure,
would be enormously flexible and powerful. Rather than organizational
structure, we might then have to talk about *organizational organisms* because this continuous "swarming" of team-like activity would resemble
real-life organisms at the cellular level. Technology would control the daily,
more automated functions, and people would focus on the new and exciting activities.

Concluding Thoughts

When management plans its strategies, often the possibilities touched on
in this chapter become lost in the shuffle. Strategies, missions, goals, organizational theory, and talk of organizational structures are all enticing.
Making decisions somehow seems much more exciting and important
when those decisions involve steering the entire organization. However, if

upper managers want to change the structure of organizational decision making, it will take more than just planning. If these managers do not convince their middle and lower managers that the change benefits them directly, then real change is unlikely.

Sometimes it seems what upper management does best is to create plans that are never implemented. It is not enough to have a vision. Managers cannot afford to sit passively and refuse to dirty their hands with the daily implementation. Upper managers who do not actually effect change are asking for trouble. Any change, including horizontal management, needs a champion. That is the task of upper management.

In order to implement a horizontal-management strategy the perceived threat must be eliminated. If status is taken away, it must be returned; however, the way this is to be done will have to change along with the structure of the organization.

Begin by changing the way people are rewarded. Reward moving laterally. Reward learning and problem solving. Reward teaching. Reward technicians on a scale equal to that of administrators.

Above all, remember, that what some see as privilege is seen by others as discrimination. All of us understand what is fair, and no one would deny those who work the hardest, but things can and do get out of hand. Equity is the key concept and excessive perks and privileges are not equitable. It is hard to ask for greater involvement and at the same time say that the old rules of privilege still apply.

Notes

1. Bill Sarorito, "The Revolt Against 'Working Smarter,'" *Fortune*, July 21, 1986, p. 60.
2. David Kirkpatrick, "Is Your Career On Track?" *Fortune*, 2 July, 1990, p. 39.
3. Ibid., p. 39.
4. Ibid., p. 39.
5. Ibid., p. 39.
6. John H. Sheridan, "Lean But Not Mean," *Industry Week*, 19 February 1990, pp. 53–56.
7. Ibid., p. 53.
8. Ibid., p. 53.
9. Ibid., p. 39.
10. "Productivity and Quality Survey," *Focus Industrial Engineering*, April 1990, p. 6.
11. "Companies Cutting Perks For Their Chief Executives," *The Washington Post*, 8 July, 1990, p. 53.
12. Kate Ballen "Let Them Eat Bread," *Fortune*, 24 September, 1990, p. 9.
13. Kirkpatrick, p. 40.

15
How Do You Begin?

B y this point you are either convinced of the need for a change or not. If you believe there is a need for a change, then there is one question that comes to mind and that is, "How do I get started?" The answer is, it depends on where you want to go and what you want to do. In other words, what do you want to accomplish?

This last chapter provides a road map and points out major junctions in the road. It will be up to you to choose which way to go. At the end of this road lies the ultimate—level one organization, but there are many alternative routes and stopping points. Before starting down this road, however, there are certain *prerequisites for change*. Without these you need not bother to begin.

Prerequisites for Change

The first of these prerequisites is *a strong reason to change*. There are some strong reasons for changing the way work is done. In Chapter 1 we reviewed many of these reasons. If they weren't enough to convince, consider these additional incentives. A decade ago 94 percent of the computers bought in the United States were made in the U.S. By 1989, that figure had dropped to 66 percent. Japan's output is already two-thirds that of America's and *growing* faster.[1]

We are losing our market share in a wide range of basic industries including automobiles, and the competition is increasing. According to Tom Peters, Germany works twelve fewer days a year than Japan but exports 2.5 times more per capita and runs an overall trade balance that exceeds Japan's.[2] Imagine the muscle when East and West Germany are fully integrated. Lost market share, especially in durable goods, is extremely difficult to recapture. The United States might even fail to retain the market share it still has.

To counteract many of these trends, many companies are adopting new ways of doing business. "Competitive pressures are forcing corporations to adopt flexible strategies and structures."[3] Competition, constant change, and the new emphasis on the customer have forced companies to become faster and more responsive. To that end, corporations have flattened and purposely pushed decision making down through the organization.[4]

Deciding What to Do

Assuming we all agree that changes need to be made, this meets our first prerequisite—motivation to change. The second is to *decide what is needed* to bring about constructive changes. Fundamental to change is the need to have a central focus. Do not "just do it"; decide what you want to do, what you really believe is essential to change things, and then head in that direction.

A good example of a company able to focus itself is Cypress Semiconductor Corporation of San Jose, California. To help them focus their efforts, they make extensive use of goals. At Cypress, each week their people set goals, commit themselves to achieving them by specific dates, and then enter the results into a common data base that reports whether they succeeded or not. Their goals are organized by project and function, with group members setting short-term goals and then ranking them by priority.[5] This way everyone knows which direction to head.

Everything works better when you know what you want to do and follow a plan. All components need to fit together. Implementing a horizontal philosophy will be far easier with a plan. To that end, Ford's Eight Step Process provides a good map for anyone contemplating change. As mentioned earlier, Ford first developed support and commitment to the idea, created a sense that both employees and management were equal partners, diagnosed what changes were needed, planned how to do it, prepared the organization for the change, and did a need's assessment to see how they measured up. This is a pretty good plan.

Measuring the Change

The last prerequisite is to have in place a system to *measure the change* before trying to change. Only then will it be possible to determine whether any change occurred. Most work is not accurately measured; all work should be. Measuring what is occurring is usually essential for change. As the adage goes, "If you can't measure it, you can't manage it." Until you have a good management system in place, you are not ready for change.

Unless you know how far along you are at implementing changes, you are just shooting in the dark. A prerequisite to change is to do what Met Life did. They first found out the effectiveness of their current horizontal communication. When they measured the gap between expectations and fact, then and only then could they determine the degree to which they were meeting those expectations.

Feedback is essential to improving the flow of work. The better, the more accurate, the more timely, and the more relevant the feedback, the better everyone understands whether changes are working as intended. Measurement is essential to evaluating this feedback. American Express's focus on measuring single customer transactions or Motorola's use of a common metric called "defect per unit" helps everyone "speak the same language." This common language is essential. It not only enhances communication flow and speed, it breaks down departmental walls and helps people understand each other.

Transformations

I do not believe long-term change can occur unless the prerequisites for change have been met. If strides have been taken in that direction, management can concentrate on specific changes needed to produce a more horizontal, flexible, and competitive organization.

As noted in Chapter 6, going from a vertical organization to a more horizontal one should be thought of as a continuum that begins at step I and goes through step V. Few, if any organizations, however, would begin at step I then proceed to step V only after each previous step had been completed. Things are just not that neat.

Depending on their circumstances, companies may need to introduce pieces and parts of each of these steps, but in no particular order. For instance, a product design team is a step V task, but it can be organized and launched before an organization fully implements reorganization of operational or step I activities.

Organizations are not equally ready for change in all areas. Conditions for change throughout an organization depend in part on the education, training, and quality of employees and managers at different levels throughout the company. Change begins slowly. Where it first occurs should depend on those areas most ready for change—those most easily transformed.

The Knowledge Gap

The first condition that must exist for change to take root is to *reduce the knowledge gap*. Knowledge, or rather the lack of it, is what makes people appear ignorant—not stupid, just ignorant. We know how smart we are, we just wonder about everyone else. As the adage goes, "If you want it done right, do it yourself." As noted earlier, about 80 percent of managers do not have a basic faith in the quality of their people.

For most of us it takes a lot of effort to trust others. There is no way managers will trust subordinates if they feel they are not smart enough to handle responsibility. One manager told me, "Stupid is for life." Well, stupidity may be for life, but ignorance is correctable. Sometimes we get those two confused.[6] Just because someone does not have the background or training does not mean they are stupid.

Most of us to one degree or another are ignorant. I am extremely ignorant when it comes to repairing a car, but many of those high school dropouts that rebuild engines for SRC might be thought of as ignorant— by the stupid. According to Stack and his management team, they know more about finance and income statements than the typical college graduate. He and the rest of his company have found that ignorance can be cured with information. The strength of SRC is grounded in his faith in his people.

In order to change to a more horizontal organization, we do not need to recruit smart people, we need to educate the people we have. As the European textile operations clearly show, our competitiveness problem is with foreign companies not paying low wages; rather, it is with foreign companies who pay higher wages than we and educate their work force. To move toward horizontal structures means moving toward greater employee responsibility and authority. If these people are not educationally prepared, no amount of managerial initiative will compensate.

In order to transform organizations into more horizontal structures, we must begin to reduce the knowledge gap between manager and worker. Where the knowledge gap is the smallest is the place where horizontal management can most easily be introduced.

Since knowledge is power, some will resist sharing it. To have truly empowered people, they must develop a wider perspective of what they do and its effect on the corporation. Specialists with narrow interests suffer from tunnel vision and have little place in horizontal structures. Specialists work in series, connected to each other. Horizontal management demands parallel thinking and processing of information. As in the case of the Pepsi General Bottlers, each member needs cross-training and multi-responsibility. Job classifications are the enemy of horizontal management and a significant barrier to full engagement of the work force.

If we are to be able to create flatter, more flexible organizations, multi-disciplined, multi-responsible people are essential. Horizontal organizations need people who have a wider understanding of all aspects of work. Training for all functions and levels must consist of exposure to a wider range of responsibilities. In essence, as organizations transform, each of us must be willing to be an apprentice.

Every organization will have to find its own way of growing into horizontal structure. Cypress uses goals as a major tool to do this. SRC uses the income statement and the balance sheet to teach each member how the business works, how to measure what goes on, and how each part fits into the larger picture. At Pepsi General Bottlers of Springfield each member of the company can do the other person's job. The Marketing can run the production plant, and the production manager could act as a marketing representative or even run the office or anything that is needed. Other companies have implemented NOAC, which also forces each person to interact and understand more than just their little specialty. There is no one best way to move to a horizontal organization; every company needs to find the system that suits their circumstances.

Partnerships

Creating a sense of multi-responsibility is one of the transformations that must occur as organizations go horizontal. This also requires that companies allow their workers a sense of *partnership* in the enterprise. Some managers are not willing to do any more in this direction than just to try to keep in touch with their workers. Perhaps these managers hope that employees will feel a sense of association because management is paying attention to them. Sometimes it works, sometimes it does not. Often it depends on whether or not those same employees see the attention as manipulation or sincere recognition.

Ultimately, management must decide whether employees will become full partners in the enterprise, for only the full partnership leads to a true horizontal organization. Anything less will not do.

A partial sense of partnership can be instilled in employees through the use of recognition and communication tools. This type of motivational approach uses horizontal network tools, but, in contrast to full partnership approaches, *does not restructure decision making.*

Full partnership actively engages a wide range of personnel in decision making; it empowers the organization rather than the employees. This seems contradictory, but it is not. Full partnership blurs the old vertical distinction of management and employee. Use of these horizontal structural motivators to this degree leads ultimately to level-one organization.

Horizontal networks, or partial-partnership organizations like Globe, are really empowered vertical organization, good ones perhaps, but vertical nevertheless. They can never become horizontal until the decision-making process is changed. Horizontal network organizations try to improve communication and motivate people by bringing them into the problem investigation and recommendation stage, but not into the decision-making process. Only be delegating actual decision making can organizations transform themselves from a vertical to a horizontal structure.

Ownership

A sense of partnership can be created by developing a sense of *ownership* within the organization—not symbolic ownership, but real ownership.

Profit sharing, ESOPs, and, more recently, PepsiCo's stock options have been used to give employees a real sense of ownership. Each of these techniques could be used by vertical and horizontal companies. While both types of companies use such plans, it is the rare case when employee stockholders actively make decisions that affect profits. Most of them do not even have a rudimentary knowledge of the financial aspects of a business. Certainly, most have no access to the data that would allow them to see direct relationships between their actions and the profits of the company. This does not imply that every corporation needs to teach all their employee stockholders the financial details as SRC has. What this does mean is that employees must make the connection between their efforts and the bottom line. Until this occurs, the transformation to a more horizontal organization will be unlikely, perhaps even impossible. If they do make the connection, it will empower vertical organizations, but it will supercharge horizontal ones.

Profit-sharing ESOPs, stock options, and other financial or stock plans are not the only way to create a sense of ownership. They are certainly not essential to create the feeling of ownership. What is essential is that management addresses the issue of *inequity.*

As noted earlier, in many companies there is a great disparity in the pay, perks, and status. There will always be differences in pay and perks, and most expect that, just as long as it is equitable. What is necessary is for those who must deliver the products and services to *feel* like they are being treated fairly. If it is true in your company, as in many others, that employees feel upper managers are reaping too much pay when compared to them—even compared to stockholders—then something has to be done. Either upper management must create an understanding of why they deserve more or provide more for those who deserve it. Either way, it helps insure the transformation toward a more horizontal structure.

Form Follows Function

Essential for a transformation to a more horizontal arrangement is, if at all possible, to eliminate lines of authority. If that is impossible, at least minimize them. In their place establish *lines of communication.* It is the work that needs to take place that should take precedence over position.

NOAC is only one approach that seeks to substitute internal customer/supplier relationships in the place of boss/subordinate relationships. Boss/subordinate relationships are unequal; customer/supplier relationships are, for they focus not on position in the pyramid, but rather on function.

You can flatten an organization by streamlining it so employees concentrate their efforts on accomplishing their true function. Many employees have not even bothered to figure out exactly what their function is. Some believe it is placating their boss. Perhaps they are right, but it should not be that way. With apologies to architect Frank Lloyd Wright, companies should be organized so that *Form Follows Function*.

To get started developing a more competitive culture, first ask yourself, "Exactly what is the purpose of my business and how can I contribute to it?" You may discover you need to reorganize it, perhaps by implementing a NOAC policy or, like American Express, by focusing on single customer transactions or, like Cypress, focus on goals. Whatever the function, organize all work around that function and do not get stuck conceptually on titles, levels, or hierarchies. Ask "What form needs to exist so we best serve our function?"

Undoubtedly, such an attitude will bring about many changes. People resist change. Some will be afraid of new responsibilities. Others will fear loss of power and control. It is essential to use *knowledge incentives* to encourage change. In vertical organizations, the incentive is moving up the pyramid. In a horizontal one, the incentive must be rewards to those who seek new responsibilities and new knowledge.

Transforming an organization to become more horizontal demands we pay for skills or knowledge acquired, not for position. The sooner we separate position and pay, the better. We often assume that those in higher positions have greater responsibility and thus greater pay; but is that always true? Is it really that logical or is it that those who determine the pay scales are simply higher in the pyramid? The correlation between position and responsibility may have been true at one time, but with the way organizations are changing today, what was once true of the skills and abilities needed to do a job may no longer be true. To become more horizontal, ask yourself this question, "Why not offer pay based on what an employee knows; measure knowledge and reward those who acquire it?" Is that the way your business runs? Should that be the way it is run?

Eliminating Impediments to Change

Creating a sense of partnership and ownership, and a feeling of empowerment is not enough to insure that change occurs. Management can create a desire to participate and expose employees to new situations and new responsibilities, but all the motivation will not help unless those same people have the tools to manage the new situation. There are plenty of them available. *Problem-solving tools* (e.g. histograms, cause-and-effect diagrams, control charts) like those used by Alcoa are good. This depends completely on your company's situation. Most important is the principle that the greater the responsibility, the greater the need for problem-solving skills and the tools to implement them.

The greatest tool of all though may not be a tool at all, at least not in the strictest sense. Foremost among problem-solving tools is the ability to *eliminate the need for making decisions*. That is the best way to improve productivity and competitiveness. As we have seen, there are many ways to do it. We could automate decisions as DuPont is trying to do with their Expert Systems. We could implement information networks. "DuPont is committed to tying all its 80 businesses in 50 countries into a uniform information network."[7] PepsiCo's most profitable division has a new network that joins the hand-held computers used by everyone of its ten thousand route salespeople to the office of company president Robert Beeby.[8]

Eliminating decisions can occur by establishing direct computer links on the shop floor, as Globe has for its customization activities. The whole concept of computer-integrated business is a hot topic as sales, finance, manufacturing, and distribution computer systems have begun to work in concert exchanging information. Customers' specifications can be sent automatically to a designer's computer-aided design system that automatically sends the customers' specifications directly to computer-aided manufacturing machines (without human intervention), which makes the product. The factory of the future, where no human has a machine-like role, is fast approaching.

Eliminating decisions is not the only way to speed transformation. *Eliminating barriers* or organizational walls between departments is essential. The essence of this new approach is to retreat from the caste system of vertical organizations that walled off marketers from engineers from production. Increasingly, companies today are experimenting with systems that they would not have thought possible a few years ago. According to Rosabeth Moss Kanter, we are seeing peers in different divisions working together in, "cross-marketing, joint purchasing, and cooperative product and market innovation."[9]

Departmental walls are not the only barriers to restructuring. Restrictive work rules and highly specialized workers create an incredible amount of inefficient compartmentalization. Rules should be based on what is physically and psychologically possible, not what is decided for political or bureaucratic reasons. Some work rules are needed, but those limited rules should be constantly challenged. Technology changes and job needs change. To fast-forward change, someone should be looking constantly at how to eliminate specialization and work rules.

Joint Decision Making

One concept essential to horizontal management is the need for joint decision making. We have already noted Ford's efforts. Groups of people everywhere are getting into the act and for good reason. The potential of *group decision making* is almost unlimited. Author Tom Peters says, "the power of the team is so great that it is often wise to violate apparent common sense and force a team structure on almost anything."[10]

Companies left and right are adopting team management as the preferred mode of operation. One case where teams are redesigning work is at Ingersoll-Rand. At one of the facilities, their compressor or needle bearings are made from beginning to end on a single plant floor and where all the machinery is operated by a cell or small team of multi-skilled workers. No longer do they assemble their product in the piecemeal assembly-line manner. Notes one manager at the facility, "The job of foreman is disappearing. Instead, team members in each cell do the whole job, tackling whatever needs to be done to meet schedules and maintain quality."[11]

However, this is not the whole story. The concept of team management within many companies has gone far beyond Ingersoll-Rand's SWG. Johnsonville Foods, Rohm and Haas Bayport, and SRC make use of teams for top management decisions. These teams are charged with authority to make decisions. Their use has become so common in some areas there are already terms like concurrent engineering to describe the process.

Clearly, teams or cells of employees will be the primary vehicle to transform companies into more horizontal ones. One cannot flatten the pyramid without them, and they are a key method of empowering people. Team management holds unlimited potential. Assuming we can learn how best to use them, anything is possible.

Level One

It may be hard to imagine anything beyond totally involving the customer, but as we have seen, there is. Despite this admirable objective, giving people a more customer-focused perspective by creating horizontal networks will, at best, only enhance communication and perhaps speed—but at great effort. Change will not be self-sustaining unless organizations restructure so that all decisions, not just those that affect the customer, focus horizontally, not vertically. As long as there are levels and bosses, then NOAC and other customer-focused techniques will only enhance communication flow; they will not change it.

This book has attempted to show the fundamental changes occurring in organizations. No one should doubt that pyramids are flattening. Few doubt that it is good for organizations. As noted earlier, it is fairly clear that teams will be a vital part of both flattening pyramids and shortening the distance of those levels that remain.

One key question remains, and that is "how flat can organizations go?" Many management experts will tell you that five levels is ideal; some say three. There are cases where there are only two levels, but is level one possible? It appears the answer is yes and no. Yes, it is possible. No, it will not happen unless we rethink some of our fundamental assumptions about organizations and leadership.

Fluid Leadership

Foremost among these vertical assumptions is the belief about the static nature of leadership. Level one is plausible if we discard assumption that there must always be only one leader, all the time, in one position. In truly flexible and adaptive organizations, one should be able to call on different parts of the organizations to make decisions based on *competency*, not on position. Sometimes these two are related; sometimes they are not. It would seem unusual to expect nonroutine decisions to involve exactly the same variables and require the same degree of expertise. Routine decisions are made by managers using procedures or machines like expert systems. Level-one leadership would seem possible if these routine decisions were properly automated and nonroutine decisions were left to decision makers.

In the future it is doubtful that most decisions will be made by individuals. Decisions are simply becoming too complex and too interdependent for any one person to have all the necessary information. Level one would seem possible if the communication network between these cells or teams of organizational entities is tight enough and comprehensive enough.

Currently, we are seeing computers increasingly being used to speed up the communication between organizational members. Today, managers can send out inquires on computer networks that are linked to colleagues around the world forming what is, in effect, a giant brain that draws on the resources needed. With this kind of capability available why does there need to be just one decision-making center all the time? My own opinion is that there doesn't.

Transparency

Each of us possesses unique competencies; systematic ways need to be found to draw on those competencies if level one is to become a reality. To make a horizontal change, *all* members of the company must become highly knowledgeable about the organization's corporate-wide needs. Organizations staffed by those people who are narrowly focused on a specialized knowledge and are working in relative isolation will not be competitive.

Given enough trust, it would seem possible for all of us to possess more comprehensive knowledge of corporate-level considerations. With sufficient information, is it unreasonable to expect that the workers would make the same decisions that management would? After all, most of the differences in decisions are based on different perceptions caused by different degrees of access to information.

Decisions are based on our perception of the problem and its causes. If the proper climate for making decisions can be established and the operational level personnel have full information, they will make equally good or equally proper decisions. They may not make the same decision as management might have made, but they will be good ones. This is the power of SRC's budgetary process. By providing employees with the facts and by trusting their intelligence and their judgement to make good decisions, SRC can get tremendous commitment along the way.

To create a completely flat organization would require that information and knowledge, either through procedures or technology, must be so readily available that for all practical purposes it is *transparent*. There can be no information filters, departmental walls, or restrictions on access to the information. This is the exact opposite of an organization structured along the lines of a military or vertical model that concentrates on restricting information to a "need to know" or "for your eyes only" basis. While all eyes may not be interested in all the information all the time, they should have access to it when needed. Flat organizations are always transparent ones.

Equity

In order to come closer to level one philosophy, we must begin to see each member of the organization as an equal. Equals in ability and in intelligence, but not in function. Members of teams, or cells, are equally important even though they serve different functions. Organizational caste systems that stratify a person's potential based on title or position are the result of pyramid thinking. Intelligence, ability, and motivation have no relationship to function. This is the way to think horizontally. Unfortunately, the other, pyramidal, type of thinking is much more common.

Have you ever noticed that it is usually those management personnel who have had no exposure to the workers who believe those workers to be unintelligent and incapable? This is why programs that train people from the ground up are so important. If the MBA does not know what shop-floor people do or what engineers do or what marketing people do, can we really expect him or her to appreciate each's importance? Exposure to each other's perspective and problems is absolutely essential to creating equality in an organization. Then when we begin to sincerely believe that, "we've got incredible people around us," we will begin creating corporations of compeers. A horizontal road map showing key junctions along the way is seen in table 15–1. It is a journey we must begin soon if we are not to be left behind in the competitive race.

Concluding Thoughts

Creating horizontal organizations can only occur if we reassess our assumptions and managerial actions. In the future, leadership must become

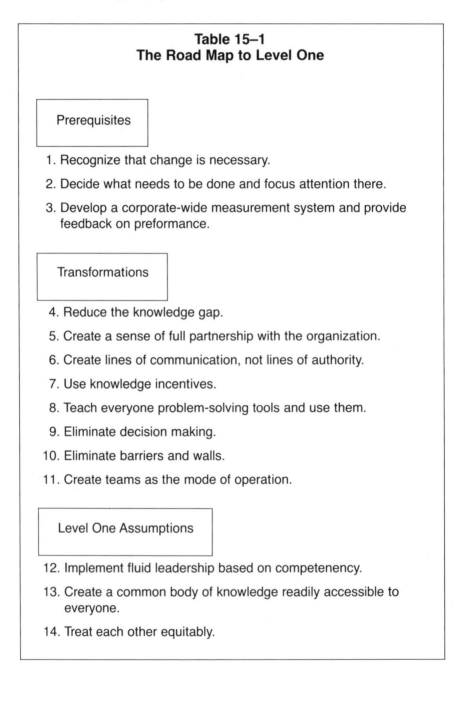

Table 15–1
The Road Map to Level One

Prerequisites

1. Recognize that change is necessary.
2. Decide what needs to be done and focus attention there.
3. Develop a corporate-wide measurement system and provide feedback on preformance.

Transformations

4. Reduce the knowledge gap.
5. Create a sense of full partnership with the organization.
6. Create lines of communication, not lines of authority.
7. Use knowledge incentives.
8. Teach everyone problem-solving tools and use them.
9. Eliminate decision making.
10. Eliminate barriers and walls.
11. Create teams as the mode of operation.

Level One Assumptions

12. Implement fluid leadership based on competenency.
13. Create a common body of knowledge readily accessible to everyone.
14. Treat each other equitably.

more fluid, the organization itself more transparent, and the way we treat each other more equitable.

It will not happen overnight. For some it will never happen, but already there are strong forces creating the need to change. In an effort to cope, companies are focusing on the customer and flattening pyramids. Organizations are trying to become more focused. NOAC is one such approach; SRC's efforts revolve around financial statements is another; and Cypress' systematic use of goals is still another way.

We will also need a better measurement system. To enhance the transformation process, there has to be a common language that all members understand and share. Motorola's defect per unit is one such language.

Having a focus and having a common way of measuring work is a start, but it takes more than measurement and mission statements. In the end these are only words; it is deeds that matter. Choose a direction for change. Reduce the knowledge gap between levels and among the departmental functions. A lack of educated employees impedes change. In the past, we did not expect too much of these people, and we could get by with that attitude. That is not the case today. Lifelong learning is not an empty slogan, it is an imperative.

Get started today by finding ways of keeping in touch with each other. I do not mean send out memos and reports or create endless red tape. All that does is kill trees. Create teams to eliminate paperwork (much of which is based on suspicion), eliminate barriers to communication, walls between departments, and restrictive work rules. Instead, find vehicles like goals, financial statements, or customer transactions as a way of staying in touch. Let everyone know what is going on, who is doing it, and what you need from them.

After you do this, then measure what you do, measure how you do it, measure the gaps between what you want and what you have. Most importantly, make sure what you measure is relevant to your goals, because what you measure is what will be important to those being measured. In horizontal organizations, you will measure and reward knowledge and skill, not position.

Once you begin to measure the right things, then work hard at giving everyone a sense of ownership. You can begin by showing trust and confidence in both those around you and below you. However, you need more than trust. Try to prepare your employees so you can accept them as equal partners. Give them more responsibility and cross-train them so they are prepared to handle change. Give them the tools to make decisions.

Trust means sharing. Ford made great strides when they accepted joint decision making. Share decision making and create teams, because those are powerful ways of improving competitiveness.

In conclusion, getting started means answering three key questions. First, "Do I have the prerequisites to change?" If not, start developing them. Second, ask, "What transformations (if any) are occurring in my organization," and "How do I speed up the process?" Finally, ask yourself, "What do I *assume* is possible?" Until you challenge those assumptions, change cannot occur.

Notes

1. Edmund Faltermayer, "Is 'Made in U.S.A.' Fading Away?" *Fortune*, 24 September, 1990, p. 62.

2. Tom Peters, "West German Management Keeps Economy Rolling," *Springfield News Leader*, XX, p. XX.

3. Rosabeth Moss Kanter, "The New Managerial Work," *Harvard Business Review*, November–December 1989, p. 85.

4. Patrick Houston, "High Anxiety," *Business Month*, June 1990, p. 34.

5. Jeremy Main, "Computers of the World Unite," *Fortune*, 24 September 1990, p. 116.

6. Kanter, p. 86.

7. Main, p. XX.

8. T. J. Rogers, "No Excuses Management," *Harvard Business Review*, July–August 1990, p. 85.

9. Kanter, p. XX.

10. Tom Peters, *Thriving on Chaos*, New York, N.Y.: Random House, 1987, p. 364.

11. Stephen Quickel, "A Company Whose Time Has Come," *Institutional Investor* 24, no. 5. (1990), pp. 107–8.

Index

About the Author

D. Keith Denton, Ph.D., is professor of management at Southwest Missouri State University. The author of eight books and over seventy management articles, he is listed in *Who's Who in America* and has been honored by numerous professional associations.